Critical Literacy
in a Digital Era

Technology, Rhetoric, and the Public Interest

Critical Literacy in a Digital Era

Technology, Rhetoric, and the Public Interest

Barbara Warnick
University of Washington

IEA LAWRENCE ERLBAUM ASSOCIATES, PUBLISHERS
2002   Mahwah, New Jersey   London

Lawrence Erlbaum Associates, Inc., Publishers
10 Industrial Avenue
Mahwah, NJ 07430

Cover design by Kathryn Houghtaling Lacey

Library of Congress Cataloging-in-Publication Data

Warnick, Barbara, 1946-
Critical literacy in a digital era : technology, rhetoric,
    and the public interest / Barbara Warnick.
    p. cm.
Includes bibliographical references and index.
ISBN 0-8058-4115-6 (cloth : alk. paper)
ISBN 0-8058-4116-4 (pbk. : alk. paper)
1. Computer literacy. I. Title.
QA76. W2395 2001
004—dc21

                                        2001033633
                                        CIP

Chapter 2, "Masculinizing the Feminine: Inviting Women Online Ca. 1997" was first published as: Warnick, B. (1999).
Masculinizing the Feminine: Inviting Women online in 1997.
Critical Studies in Mass Communication, 16, 1–19. Copyright by
the National Communication Association, 1999. Reproduced
by permission of the publisher.

Books published by Lawrence Erlbaum Associates are printed
on acid-free paper, and their bindings are chosen for strength
and durability.

Printed in the United States of America
10 9 8 7 6 5 4 3 2 1

Contents

Preface vii

Introduction: Rhetoric and Critical Literacy 1
    Critical Literacy 6
    Technology Issues and Media Policy 8
    Public Awareness and Media Literacy 10
    Rhetorical Criticism as Analytic Method 14

1 The "New Frontier" in Cyberspace: *Wired* at Work 19
    New Libertarianism: The Ideology of *Wired* 23
    The Writing Formula: A Set Piece 28
    Association and Dissociation—"Style"
    as a Form of Argument 39
    Race, Gender, and *Wired* 45
    The New *Wired*: A Change in Character? 50
    Bill Joy on the Future: A Signal Event 56
    Conclusion 59

2 Masculinizing the Feminine:
  Inviting Women Online ca. 1997 63
    Hierarchical Appeals in Invitational Discourse 67
    Converting the Uninitiated: Appeals
    in Print Media 71
    Cybergrrl Discourse on the Web 78

The Web's Changing Nature: E-Zines
and Other Alternatives 82

Conclusion 85

3 Parody With a Purpose: Online Political
Parody in the 2000 Presidential Campaign 87

Political Participation and the World Wide Web 90

Bush–Gore Parody Sites: "Saying" Something
While Saying Nothing 95

Textuality: Controlling the Reader's Point
of View 104

The Changing Political Web: Parody in 1996
and 2000 108

Conclusion 111

Conclusion: Whom Does Technology Serve? 115

Deliberation and Its Absence 116

Rhetorical Response: The Need
for a Counternarrative 120

References 129

Author Index 139

Subject Index 143

Preface

This book is written for teachers, students, and members of the general reading public who are interested in how persuasive discourse about technology affects how we think about it. Much of the writing about communication technology in the popular media tacitly subscribes to a utopian vision of how the Internet and the Web will improve our lives, lighten our work, strengthen the economy, and lead to other positive outcomes. The aim of this book is to examine the persuasive strategies used in discourse on and about the Internet. It makes use of a critical literacy framework that is built on the principle that everyone should, insofar as possible, become aware of what is assumed, unquestioned, and naturalized in our media experience.

In regard to discourse about new technologies, we need to consider what claims are credible, what evidence is accurate, and which spokespersons are truly acting in the public interest. We also should recognize explicitly how advocates and writers use narratives, myths, forms of language, and visual images to tell their stories. Through critical examination of these features, we can begin to see what ideologies are at work and whose interests are being served by the discourse. This is an important step to a thorough understanding of the issues at stake in the formation of technology policy and of how decisions on these issues may affect us and our lives. My hope, then, is that this book will play a role in the development of critical literacy about writing and speech concerning new communication technology.

I first became interested in studying the Internet as a communication medium in 1996 when I attended the Depauw Undergraduate Honors Conference in communication as a guest speaker. Dozens of young people from colleges and universities throughout the United States were in attendance, and it seemed like many of them spent most of their conversation time talking with each other about technology. Some were their department's Webmasters or technical support staff. Others were interested in the Internet as a social phenomenon and in how it affected their schoolwork and personal lives. Although I had used the Internet for some time, I had not realized the extent to which the rise of the World Wide Web was affecting young people and changing their lives.

At the same conference, a colleague recommended that I read Turkle's (1995) *Life on the Screen: Identity in the Age of the Internet*. Turkle thoughtfully considered many ways that computer technology affects how we think about ourselves, interact with other people, form communities, and construct our personal identities. Reading her book made me aware of the profound impact of new technologies and online communication on our lives.

It also became clear to me that not much work was being done by humanist scholars in communication on the rhetorical aspects of the Internet and the Web. The web-based *Journal of Computer-Mediated Communication* had been formed in 1995, and in that journal and others, social science researchers considered patterns of relationship development, interpersonal communication, group formation, gender differences, and other aspects of interaction in online environments. However, as the Web took shape and much of its content seemed contrived for rhetorical purposes, it seemed to me that study of its patterns of influence and persuasion were called for.

I decided that studying the persuasive features of Internet-related discourse was intriguing and of significance to communication study, and thus began my own work by studying political parody Web sites in the 1996 Presidential campaign. At that time, the Web was still fairly disorganized, and parody sites were cacophonous, irreverent, and amateurish. Nevertheless, the parodic Web sites proved to be very interesting rhetorically, as parody provides commentary and makes allusions that would not be permitted in more traditional media environments.

During this same period, I also became interested in how and why the Internet seemed to be such a gendered environment. In the early 1990s, its content, preoccupations, and publications seemed to offer little of interest to women. Much of the writing about gender and the Internet at that time argued that women were marginalized, harassed, or ignored in online communication. Yet the advent of the Web and its growth as a mass medium meant that the stakes involved in getting women online were high. In examining the persuasive strategies used in women's magazines, gateway Web sites, and other venues addressed to women, I found that much of this discourse exhorted women to get involved with technology or reproached them for having failed to do so. This hardly seemed likely to succeed as an invitational strategy.

My work on this topic was published in 1998 in the journal *Critical Studies in Mass Communication* and is included here as chapter 2. This historical account of women's online experiences describes a key phase in the development of the World Wide Web. Women now make up more than half of people coming on line, and they do so because there are good reasons for them to use what the Web now has to offer. They have taken possession of their sector of online communication. Whether they use the Internet to communicate with family and friends, seek social support, or gather information on fitness, sports, fashion, or women's issues, their patterns of use thrive in equal proportion to those of their male counterparts. Chapter 2 tells part of the story of women's arrival online, and it indicates how their presence has contributed to subsequent changes in the nature of the Web itself.

The rest of the chapters in this book report the continuing story of discourse on and about the Internet. Chapter 1 considers another form of protechnology advocacy—the writings that have appeared in *Wired* magazine. Since its initial publication in 1993, *Wired* has been the only mass-circulation magazine designed to report on cutting edge, computer-based communication technology and to appeal to that sector of the

public preoccupied with Internet-related communication issues. *Wired* is therefore a site of great interest to the rhetorician
who wants to study persuasive discourse about new communication technology. Chapter 3 extends my 1996 study by considering political parody on the Web in the 2000 presidential
campaign. Comparing the 2000 Web parodies with those in
1996 provides a snapshot of how persuasion on the Web has
changed as the medium itself has become more organized,
more structured, and more commercial.

This book would not have been completed without the support and assistance of many individuals. I would like to thank
my research assistants for their contributions and the University of Washington for providing funding and support for their
work. Scott Lybarger and Jennifer Peeples assisted with the collection of information and materials in the early phases of my
work on gender and political parody online. Their highly com-
petent work ensured inclusion of the pertinent articles and
Web sites that I studied. In the past year, I have been assisted by
Sophie McDowell and Jason Edward Black who shared my interest in protechnology discourse and political parody. Sophie
was one of the fastest and most efficient database researchers
with whom I have worked. Jason's thoroughness and lively interest in the political scene added new perspective and value to
my study on parody in the 2000 presidential campaign.

I would also like to thank the reviewers of the work included
here. Gerald J. Baldasty of the School of Communications at
Washington offered a number of valuable comments on chapter 1. Stuart Kaplan of Lewis and Clark College and Lawrence
Mullin of the University of Nevada Las Vegas provided useful
comments on chapter 3. Laura Gurak of the University of Minnesota read the entire book, and her marginal comments and
review as a whole were exceedingly helpful as I revised the
book for publication. I also benefited from the fine work of
Lawrence Erlbaum Associates' reviewers, Carolyn Miller of
North Carolina State University and Christine Miller of California State University Sacramento.

Linda Bathgate, Communications Editor at Lawrence
Erlbaum Associates, has been interested in and enthusiastic

about this project throughout the review process. She has also worked to develop a time-sensitive project into a book very competently and efficiently, and I am grateful to her for her support. I must also thank my husband, Michael R. O'Connell, who has always been generous with his own knowledge of computer systems and his support of my work.

—*Barbara Warnick*

Introduction: Rhetoric and Critical Literacy

The contemporary media scene is heavily populated by magazines, books, and other publications that offer up scenarios about our technology future. Predictions that might have been dismissed as outrageous or impossible 20 years ago have recently become unsurprising. For example, Kurzweil (1999) in his book *The Age of Spiritual Machines*, predicted that by 2019, a $1,000 computing device will "equal the computational ability of the human brain" (p. 278); by 2029, the "majority of communication [will] not involve a human [and] the majority of communication involving a human [will be] between a human and a machine" (p. 279); and by 2099, there will be "a strong trend toward a merger of human thinking with the world of machine intelligence ... and no longer any clear distinction between humans and computers" (p. 280). Because this author was inventor of the Kurzweil Reading Machine in 1976, the developer of the first commercially marketed speech recognition system in 1987, and recipient of the National Medal of Technology in 1999, many of his readers took his views quite seriously. His book—a series of predictions supported by accounts of the history of technology development, examples of current scientific research, and descriptions of future time—did not at first attract widespread media attention or criticism, however.

At about the same time that Kurzweil's book appeared, *Wired* magazine, a general periodical written for the technoliterate, published a special issue on the future. In it, the magazine's executive editor, Kevin Kelly, made a set of prognostications nearly as

1

startling as Kurzweil's. Kelly speculated that a long boom of ultraprosperity might be in store for Americans. If computing and other forms of technology development continued unabated, there would be no end in sight for incremental improvements in lifestyle and personal wealth.

Kelly imagined the Dow at 50,000 by 2010, an average household income of $150,000 (with no inflation), 75% of household income free for nonessentials, and, through free market forces, the elimination of poverty in America (Kelly, 1999).[1] Certain conditions would be necessary for this to occur. These included "the spread of democracy, open markets, freedom of speech, and consumer choice around the globe" (p. 151). These conditions would attract investment capital and money from outside the United States.

> If ultra prosperity blooms, huge waves of money will continue to flow into U.S. stock markets and startups as the best deals on Earth.... That giant sucking sound you hear is all the world's money rushing into the most booming economy. In the vortex, money is well treated, multiplying fast, sucking in yet more money. (Kelly, 1999, p. 154)

Kelly concluded his article by observing that, to the extent that American ultraprosperity might stimulate competition, other regions of the world might also benefit economically.

Also in 1999, the magazine *Scientific American* published an issue on the future of computing. One contributing writer was Michael L. Dertouzos, Director of the MIT Laboratory for Computer Science. He predicted that computing technology "will be able to increase human productivity by 300 percent [during the 21st century] as we automate routine office activities and offload brain and eyeball work onto our electronic bulldozers" (Dertouzos, 1999, p. 52). Noting that at the time of his writing, the 100 million interconnected computers represented

---

[1]Whether Kelly's predictions are remotely possible will only be known in time. In the meantime, the early months of 2001 showed all the signs of a possible recession and a sharp drop in values of stocks, particularly technology stocks (Howe, 2001).

only 1.6% of the world's population, Dertouzos imagined technology's capacity to make life better for all of humanity. He described a "Virtual Compassion Corps" that could make health care and other services cheaply available to the poor worldwide by means of technology, as well as use of the Internet to purchase and sell information work. "Imagine," he concluded, "1,000 accountants from Beijing doing accounting services for General Motors at $1 per hour" (p. 54).

Predictions such as these are of interest to those of us who study the persuasive features of public discourse. What is it about these writings that appeals to the public and receives steady attention in the popular press? Why is it that protechnology discourse seems to find a ready audience, cells of enthusiastic supporters, and so little sustained opposition in the public sphere? The case studies in this book are designed in part to answer such questions. Intense optimism at the onset of technological breakthroughs is surely not a new phenomenon, but there are some unusual and unique aspects to the most recent variant of it as reflected in the writings of Kurzweil, Kelly, and Dertouzos.[2]

A rhetorical analyst examining these works would see some noticeable patterns in the ways in which these men appeal to their audiences. They address their readers as one addresses true believers—people who already subscribe to the premises on which they base their predictions. For example, readers who are in the know about new computing technology are familiar with Moore's Law, which holds that the number of transistors on a single computer chip will double every 18 months for the foreseeable future (S. E. Miller, 1996).[3] This geometrical increase in microchip power allows for exponential increases in computing capacity and commensurate potential for computing-based technology development. If one works out the mathematics of this principle, the supplanting

---

[2]For accounts of the enthusiasm that has accompanied the advent of new communication technologies in the past, see S. E. Miller (1996) and Marvin (1987).

[3]Gordon Moore, Chairman of Intel, predicted this geometrical increase in microchip power, which results in an annual growth rate of 60%. This is a major reason computers become progressively more powerful and less expensive as time passes.

of human by machine intelligence can come to seem entirely possible and even reasonable.

Another component of persuasion in such predictive discourses is their appeal to readers' desires for economic and social advancement. In terms of the social commentary of Burke (1950), people are drawn to the mysteries of new technology and technical expertise. Computer scientists, genetics researchers, and technology developers are frequently viewed as harbingers of innovations that will lead to economic development and an elevated standard of living. Burke noted that the "hierarchic principle"—the desire to transcend one's present condition and move upward in the social hierarchy—"is inevitable in systematic thought" (p. 141). The promise of nearly unlimited technological advancement implies the potential for continuous self- and social improvement and upward mobility. When accompanied by presumptions that the United States is the most powerful country in the world, that it functions as the center of development for new technology applications, and that its free market economy is the best environment in which to cultivate technology innovation, many of the predictions in protechnology discourse can be powerfully appealing.

As chapter 1 of this book indicates, those who foresee phenomenal developments in computing technology often address their audiences as if such future developments are inevitable and even foreordained. If Moore's Law continues to hold true and our technological capacity does indeed accelerate exponentially over time, then the creation of virtual environments, diminution of human-to-human contact, and relegation of work and labor entirely to computing devices appear to be logical outcomes. One problem with inevitability, however, is that it precludes deliberation. These experts' reliance on historical trajectories of scientific development, predictive pronouncements, and, most of all, their own specialized, technical expertise disqualifies the lay reader from discussions about technology development (W. R. Fisher, 1987).

Additional reasons for the broad appeal of protechnology rhetoric were insightfully identified by C. R. Miller (1994) when she examined images and models of technological change in such discourse. These images depended on metaphors that gained their presumptive force from habits of thought prevalent in Western society. For example, the idea of "generations" of technology suggests necessary change over time and a successive progression of increasingly complex and sophisticated technical capacities. Spatial metaphors (the "spread ... of consumer choice," a technological "breakthrough," a "window of opportunity," etc.) orient readers' thinking toward expansion of a territory (another hierarchically motivated mode of thought). Temporal metaphors characterizing technology development as a "race" and change as progressively "accelerated" have the same effect (p. 86). Miller concluded that several features of protechnology discourse "add up to an implicit self-justifying argument" (p. 89) the final step of which is "to validate forecasting by making it come true, to turn the description of the future into the construction of the future, prediction into control" (p. 90).

Observers who have worried over the public's lack of attention to and engagement in major issues such as technology development have noted public apathy, indifference, and ambivalence about the social effects of technology policy (Bellah, Madsen, Sullivan, Swidler, & Tipton, 1996; McChesney, 1999; S. E. Miller, 1996). However, the public does attend to technology issues, particularly to those related to antitrust litigation, Internet security, and regulation of free speech. In addition, many media sectors emphasize and promote new media and computing technology development. These include trade books such as Rheingold's (1993) *The Virtual Community*, Gates's (1995) *The Road Ahead*, Sinclair's (1996) *Net Chick*, and Tapscott's (1998) *Growing Up Digital*. Magazines such as *Wired* and *Mondo2000* have been consumed by a large sector of the reading public. Other commercial media, including newspapers, television, and the World Wide Web, attend closely to technology development and its effects on society.

If the reading, viewing, and browsing publics unquestioningly buy into the predictions and tacit ideologies in this media discourse, then the beliefs and values embedded in it will not be subject to public discussion and critical examination. One solution proposed for this problem is development of critical literacy in citizens and particularly in students. Defined by Tyner (1998) as "a deeper kind of literacy" (p. 30) than alphabetic or media literacy, critical literacy refers to the ability to stand back from texts and view them critically as circulating within a larger social and textual context. Critical literacy in part means communicating about communication. It includes the capacity to look beneath the surface of discourse, to understand implicit ideologies and agendas, to think and speak for oneself, to understand how social contexts affect how texts are designed and understood, and to appreciate the resources of cultural and linguistic diversity (Gurak, 2001; New London Group, 1996).

This book aspires to contribute to critical thinking about public issues related to technology development. Its aims are to examine how certain values, such as progress, profit and access to information, are elevated in such public discourse, whereas others, such as community and social justice, are displaced. By considering how the spokespersons of the technological elite seek to influence their audiences, this book draws attention to who is allowed to speak, under what conditions, and to what ends. By disclosing the beliefs and values embedded in protechnology discourse, critical analysis of the discursive strategies used by protechnology advocates can make them available for public discussion and debate. It can ask how such meanings and values become sedimented, how the narratives that promote them come to be a cultural dominant, and how they are disseminated so widely and with such success.

CRITICAL LITERACY

Critical literacy has been described as a literacy that encourages a reflective, questioning stance toward the forms and content of print and electronic media (Tyner, 1998). This is an overarching term, and its benefit is to include all the forms, modalities, and devices of communication. As I use it in this book, I intend it to be inclusive, covering aural and oral literacy, information literacy, media literacy, and visual literacy. As Tyner has explained, however, each of these forms of literacy and their definitions have been highly contested by various groups and interests. It is therefore important to explain briefly the forms of literacy that make up what has been called a *multiliteracies framework* (New London Group, 1996) and to place rhetorical criticism—the approach in this book—in relation to them.

Aural and oral literacy, often viewed as originating in preliterate cultures and connected to listening, performance, public speaking, and interpersonal communication, incorporate specific abilities and competencies (Chesebro & Bertelsen, 1996; Ong, 1982). These include reception and production skills such as accurate and empathic listening, knowing and adapting to one's audience, skillful verbal expression, and clarity of communication. Information literacy refers to the ability to identify, find, evaluate, and use information (Tyner, 1998). It includes distinguishing primary from secondary information, checking content accuracy, determining the source of information, and otherwise assessing the credibility and quality of information resources. Media literacy involves understanding how media represent and construct what they depict, what media techniques are used, what effects are produced, and how media products are created (Bolter & Grusin, 1999; Hobbs, 1998; Kubey, 1998).

Rhetorical criticism complements all of these forms of literacy insofar as each of them is concerned with the social construction of meaning through symbolic action. It focuses on making the invisible (what is transparent and unnoticed) visible. Rhetorical criticism is concerned with how messages are designed for audiences and how they are intended to have an effect. By considering how language and images are used to privilege some elements while neglecting others, rhetorical criticism can make implicit ideologies explicit. By considering how messages position or "hail" their readers and viewers, rhetorical criticism discloses the assumptions authors hold about their audiences (Althusser, 1972; Butler, 1997). It can examine how message content can contribute to or detract from source credibility and how communities of interest are constructed through shared values and ways of speaking. Rhetorical criticism complements media literacy in particular, because it offers a way to examine how media messages are designed for certain groups, why some media texts might be more effective than others, what issues are raised by media coverage, and whose interests are served by media content.

TECHNOLOGY ISSUES AND MEDIA POLICY

Among scholars who have studied public discourse on and about new communication media, some have identified its rhetorical attributes, and in particular the narrative that threads together public beliefs about technology. Selfe (1999) and McChesney (1999) noted that the major elements of this narrative are faith in science, emphasis on U.S. preeminence, and reliance on unregulated free market forces as a solution to most of the world's economic problems. Selfe argued that this narrative grows out of modernism's view that science and technology, grounded as they are in systematic observation, rigor, and technological tools, will yield a better world for the human species. She emphasizes the importance of "a belief in science as a progressive force in modern society" that characterizes Western thinking in general (Selfe, 1999, p. 115). This belief is closely associated with the view that new technologies enable the United States to maintain its role as a global leader. When technology development and capitalist enterprise are combined with democratic social systems (it is thought), their potential for improving people's lives can be fulfilled. Many Americans thus believe "that they are obligated, as citizens of a progressive nation, to provide inhabitants of less fortunate countries with the social, economic, and technological resources they need in order to succeed in the same ways that Americans have done" (p. 119). Selfe labeled this ideological equation technology + democracy (+ capitalism) = progress.[4]

---

[4]This same phenomenon is discussed by Bolter and Grusin (1999), who noted:

> That digital media can reform and even save society reminds us of the promise that has been made for technologies throughout much of the twentieth century: it is a peculiarly, if not exclusively, American promise. American culture seems to believe in technology in a way that European culture, for example, may not.... In America ... collective (and perhaps even personal) salvation has been thought to come through technology rather than through political or even religious action. (pp. 60–61)

In a recently published study of media practices and public policy in America, media critic McChesney (1999) made observations similar to Selfe's. He identified hypercommercialism and the cooptation of journalism by media conglomerates as major causes of the public's lack of awareness about concentration of media ownership and control. He pointed out that a few media corporations, such as Time Warner, Disney, Viacom, Seagram's, General Electric, and AT&T, control most of the media content in the United States. These companies make sure that their products and programs are cross-advertised in the media markets where they have a presence. Because news stories and features often cover new product releases and technology ventures, "it has become increasingly difficult to distinguish editorial from explicitly commercial fare, even from advertising" (p. 35).

McChesney (1999) had few kind words to say about the idea that market forces alone should regulate the Internet. The promoters of this idea apparently believe that combining the market with the Internet allows entrepreneurs to develop new products, form companies, and compete. Competition encourages innovation and provides a cornucopia of choices for consumers. Implied in this scenario is an open and accessible Internet available to anyone who wants a voice and a place in the new economy. McChesney noted:

> These are very powerful claims about the market. It is ironic that as the claims about the genius of the market have grown in conventional discourse over the past two decades, the need to provide empirical evidence for the claims has declined. The market has assumed mythological status, becoming a totem to which all must pledge allegiance or face expulsion to the margins.... As this mythology is the foundation for almost the entire case for the absence of any public debate on the course of the Internet, and therefore in favor of the privatization and commercialization of the Internet, it demands very careful scrutiny. (p. 137)

As shown in chapter 1, the emphasis on deregulation, entrepreneurship, innovation, new product development, and trickle-down prosperity are trademarks of a political ideology known as the *new libertarianism*, a system of beliefs and values to which many members of the technological elite subscribe. The view earlier expressed by *Wired*'s Kevin Kelly that laissez-faire economics and open market practices are what conduce to uncontrolled prosperity is an example of this view. McChesney's study of the concentration of corporate capital in the hands of a powerful few reveals the problematic nature of such libertarian claims.

Along with other authors (Castells, 1996; Dawson & Foster, 1998; S. E. Miller, 1996), McChesney (1999) believed there should be greater public involvement in new media policy. Major decisions are continually made in the government and private sectors about how the Internet will be regulated, the extent to which concentrated media interests will serve the public, the forms of media infrastructure, and other matters. Because the public does not presently have a substantial influence on these decisions, McChesney argued, "the exact contours of global Internet governance will be determined in the next few years, probably with little or no public awareness or participation" (p. 134). He called for media reform and believed that citizens should come together to study technological possibilities and desired social goals for new communication technologies.

PUBLIC AWARENESS AND MEDIA LITERACY

A major barrier to media reform and citizen involvement in media-related policy, however, is the lack of awareness by many of us about the nature, content, and effects of new media. As people depend more and more on cell phones, laptops, hand-held computers, and other devices, the media forms they use may become naturalized, taken for granted, and unnoticed. As Tapscott (1998) observed, "As new media grows in connectivity, content, applications, and user population, a new kind of transparency is emerging" (p. 39). (Transparency is a condition in which the user forgets or is unaware of the presence of the medium.) Communication technology comes to be taken as a given to be used (Jordan, 1999), and its role in shaping our lives and consciousnesses becomes less visible. Mantovani (1996) maintained that,

> The less mediation is detected, because the medium is taken as equivalent to the "natural" one, the more mediated experience is surreptitiously presented and tacitly accepted as direct experience … without people becoming aware of the ways in which mediation works. (p. 124)

The naturalization and transparency of media representations can problematize the sort of public deliberation about media policy called for by McChesney (1999).

For example, chapter 1 of this book describes numerous instances in which photographs and articles in *Wired* magazine stereotyped or stigmatized ethnic groups and women. Jamieson (2000) showed how media reports of polling results subsequently influenced voters' own choices, and in earlier work (Jamieson, 1992), she used focus groups to demonstrate that viewers could not differentiate the content of political advertisements from the content of news coverage. Because of such features as digital pastiche, source anonymity, and fan out, some forms of new media are particularly prone to fool and mislead those users who cannot distinguish between facts and "real news" on one hand and fabrications on the other.[5] As reported in chapter 3, some visitors to political parody sites mistook them for the official sites posted by the candidates' campaign organizations. It is also frequently the case that rumor, gossip, and innuendo are widely disseminated and rarely questioned in new media forums (Warnick, 1998a). Citizens who are alerted to the idea that all media representations are constructions will be more inclined to distinguish between advertising and news, detect media stereotyping, recognize digital manipulation, and question the legitimacy of anonymous or vaguely authored Web sites. They will be less likely to view me-

---

[5]"Fan out" refers to the practice by which electronic texts and Internet site addresses are forwarded to address lists and newsgroups. This enables wide, instantaneous dissemination of some Internet content.

dia content as unproblematic and better prepared to consider media effects and media-related public policy and reform.

Some of the unique potential for new media in particular to operate in ways often unnoticed by their users has been discussed by various scholars. For example, Turkle (1995) observed many people's interaction with computers. As a psychologist, she was primarily concerned about how computer-mediated communication affects people's sense of self and society. She noted how gender switching and use of multiple identities provide experiences of interaction more virtual than real. She considered the extent to which gaming and online role playing may substitute for real-life experience, as well has how individuals are socialized through human–computer interaction. Doheny-Farina (1996) argued that electronic communities were an inadequate substitute for real offline communities marked by geographic proximity and long-term association. In considering the effects of computer-mediated environments on communication, he emphasized the comparative uncertainty of information found there, as well as the tendency to favor speed and imagery over argument.

Gurak (1997) used a rhetorical critical approach to examine text-based discussion in listservs, newsgroups, and e-mail. She studied how ethos (source credibility) was formed in environments where participants knew and judged each other only through text-based messages. She also considered how structures of online communication—the timing of messages, the patterns of their dissemination, and the anonymity of the source—affected the outcome of social protest online. Jordan (1999) studied forms of communication and events occurring in online environments to illustrate the ways in which power ("cyberpower") circulates in online virtual societies, particularly in relation to identity, media policy, and social formations. He contemplated how the use of certain metaphors (e.g., "the new frontier") have naturalized certain tacit understandings about the Internet (e.g., "a place imagined as available for possession"). He also described past and future instances of online victimization and abuse, such as the now-famous cyber-rape of a participant in a Net-based MOO (Multi-user Object Oriented). Jordan contemplated the potential for total surveillance made possible by computer databases that enable deposit tracking, examination of bank activity, retinal scans, and vehicle registration. By exploring the rhetorical workings of public discourse about communication technology and speech contained in on-line environments, this book extends and complements the work of these earlier theorists. It makes use of qualitative descriptive methods—primarily textual readings—to examine how such instances of communication are designed. Because it centers on case studies of rhetorical communication, this book differs from social commentary as provided by Jordan (1999) and Doheny-Farina (1996) and social psychology as practiced by Turkle (1995). It aligns with Gurak's (1997) study of text-based interaction on listservs and newsgroups but focuses instead on writings in general periodicals and on World Wide Web sites designed for large audiences.

By analyzing narrative structure, patterns of emphasis and neglect, use of genres, argument forms, intertextual relations, and figures of speech, this book explains how writers, parodists, and advocates attempt to influence audiences. Among other findings, the book illustrates how these authors exploit the features of the electronic medium, the attitudinal predispositions of the readers, and certain unchallenged cultural myths to design messages that are effective in eliciting desired responses. This sort of rhetorical critical analysis is well suited to study how language and symbols are used in social contexts because it examines how media shape meanings and influence opinions through their use of situated textual appeals.

As I have noted, rhetorical analysis of media messages supports other forms of literacy vital to an informed and educated public. For example, media literacy is often thought of in part as the ability to ascertain the effects of media messages on audiences—for example, the effects of television violence on children or exposure to political ads on voter behavior (Hobbs, 1998). Media researchers often use survey research and other means of data collection to learn how audiences actually re-

spond to media content. Rhetorical analysis of the sort offered
here, however, considers how authors and producers of messages construct or address their audiences in the text. What beliefs, values, and assumptions have they assumed their readers
hold? What sorts of received wisdom and commonplace
"truths" can they take for granted in their message design? Although survey results and quantitative analysis are vital to understanding media effects, critical analyses of message texts are
equally important. The strain of rhetorical criticism that contributes to critical literacy recognizes that a good deal of media
content is also persuasive in nature and needs to be studied as
argument. Once media have been accessed and information obtained, one must step back and inquire into their sources' motives, ideology, and underlying values. By examining the
ideological subtext implied in the metaphors, narratives, and
patterns of emphasis and neglect in discourse concerned with
new communication technology, the studies included in this
book clarify some of these tacit but unspoken messages.

RHETORICAL CRITICISM AS ANALYTIC METHOD

Rhetorical criticism as applied to oral speech and print texts often has considered the function of a single identifiable author or
speaker, a stable text, and an audience of people whose responses could be tracked and described (Warnick, 1998b). In
contrast, the analyses in this book are usually directed at more
diffuse textual environments of circulating media discourses. In
these environments, authorship is a function of groups who
conjointly produce texts based on shared ideology, values, and
interests. By virtue of certain features, these texts are interconnected to produce unique discursive domains (Mitra, 1999). For
example, the cybergrrl discourse examined in chapter 2
emerged from a related series of magazine articles, Web sites,
and advice books produced by a group of authors who shared a
certain postfeminist, technosavvy identity. The political parody sites studied in chapter 3 were organized and clustered by
networks of hypertext links and intertextual allusions.

These textual environments are decentered and yet held together by various forms of structural or content-oriented reciprocity. The case studies in this book consider how these clusters of texts refract and play off of each other, as well as how their writers position themselves and hail readers that they assume to share their values. This form of criticism is partially predicated on the idea that "the glue that holds the Internet together is the text exchanged by different users of the Internet" (Mitra & Cohen, 1999, p. 181). If many forms of identity, community, and culture are text based, then it makes sense to read components of communication *out of the text.* How do authors build their credibility through textual cues? How do they construct and shape their audiences through strategic use of shared beliefs and premises? How do they make use of narrative structures, hypertext links, textual appropriation, and parody for rhetorical effect?

Rhetorical criticism as applied in these case studies facilitates the process of critical framing that enables readers and the public to reflect on the implications of some of the forms of advocacy to which they are exposed. The New London Group (1996) defined critical framing (an important component of critical literacy) as the ability of audiences and readers to "gain the necessary personal and theoretical distance from what they have learned, constructively critique it, account for its cultural location, [and] creatively extend and apply it ... within old communities and in new ones" (p. 87).

Such criticism proceeds by observing how writers make use of text-based resources available to them and evident in the design of their messages. It studies symbolic action as carried out through visual images, specialized argots, hypertext patterns, and other means used to form identity and community. Although the focus here is on language use, many of these features are also similarly manifest in visual display and audio and could be used to study rhetorical appeals in multimedia environments.

The discursive resources considered in these studies include style, genre, and argument form. Style (the configuration of semiotic features in a text) includes the reservoir of figures of speech and syntactical forms used to evoke response. Genres (forms of textual organization or communication patterns) include exhortation, parodic commentary, epideictic speech, and predictive narrative. *Forms of argument* include argument from model (use of a central figure as exemplar to be emulated), dissociation (disengagement and hierarchical ordering of concepts), and analogy.

Text-based criticism is, of course, concerned primarily with what is going on in the message text. This does not assume, however, that information about actual audience reception and response are considered unimportant or irrelevant. This book acknowledges the importance of textual context by considering media commentary, reader reactions, reviews, and textual responses where appropriate. Further study of the ways in which media messages are received, taken up, or rejected therefore complements and adds to the text-focused studies done here.

Chapter 1 considers advocacy as recently practiced by the writers and editors of *Wired* magazine. With a readership of over one-half million, this magazine plays an influential role in the thinking of its subscribers and some segments of the public. Since its inception, the publication has covered developments in communication technology, advertised related products, and predicted future developments in the technological arena. By studying the writing formulae, narrative structures, argument forms, and patterns of emphasis and neglect in the magazine's articles, chapter 1 concludes that *Wired*'s discourse is largely ceremonial and laudatory rather than deliberative. The magazine celebrates creativity and entrepreneurship, and its tacit ideology is largely new libertarian. Since coming under new ownership in 1998, *Wired* has become more inclusive in its coverage, but both its editorial board and its reportage remain disproportionately weighted toward male and Caucasian readers. The chapter concludes with the observation that, if the magazine's recent trend toward more balance in criticizing technology and appealing to a wider range of readers continues, it might contribute meaningfully to public discussion about technology policy.

Chapter 2 examines discourses addressed to women that appeared in the early and mid-1990s in trade periodicals and gateway Web sites. At that time, the Internet population was predominately male, and many invitations to women to come online exhorted them to move forward, experiment with technology, and set their fears aside. These appeals tacitly valued aggressiveness, opportunism, and technical proficiency. They used narrative constructions, role models, dissociation, and other rhetorical strategies in efforts to persuade women to experiment with Internet communication. Female participation remained at relatively low levels, however, until many women found good reason to come online. By the late 1990s, newcomers to the Internet were evenly divided between males and females. This chapter, which deals with issues of access, community, and use, is a historical study of early female involvement in the Internet.

Chapter 3 examines a set of political parody sites that played a role in the 2000 presidential campaign and compares them with parody sites in the 1996 campaign. After briefly examining the controversy surrounding the Internet's role in U.S. politics, the chapter shows how the 2000 Bush–Gore parody site authors constructed a discursive enclave visited by the like-minded who shared the sites' political values. Unlike the 1996 sites that were eclectic, disorganized, and largely unrelated to each other, the Bush–Gore parody sites were designed to keep their readers on the site or visiting other sites in the group. Site authors accomplished this through use of common sources, intertextual allusions, networked links, and intersite redundancies. These features constructed a reader that was "in the know" and capable of appreciating the lateral cross-references. The chapter concludes by arguing that as use of the Web has spread and become a medium with a larger reach and greater profits to be made, the nature of many of its sectors has been modified. Formerly free and open communication environments have become constrained by copyright laws, search engine practices, and the need for financing.

These trends have made the Web a more strategically rhetorical environment.

By considering the patterns of exclusion, utopian narratives, and moral relativism that frequently characterize online and protechnology discourse, this book applies rhetorical critical methods to mediated discourse relevant to issues in the public sphere. Although public involvement in new media policy formation is beneficial, people's current reactions to technology development too often take the form of silence, nostalgia, or dire prediction. One way of sorting through technology-related issues is to examine what people say and do when they talk and think about communication technology or when they use it. To the extent that such discourse constructs group identities, promotes ideologies, attracts audiences, and serves particular interests, its assumptions can be made available for critical reflection and examination.

CHAPTER ONE

The "New Frontier" in Cyberspace: *Wired* at Work

In the mid-1980s, an Internet community formed in cyberspace. Titled the Whole Earth 'Lectronic Link (WELL), this group's history has been chronicled by various writers (Rheingold, 1993; Weise, 1996). The WELL became a large computer service with many groups of subscribers. Among them were what Rheingold (1993) labeled that "the personal computer revolutionaries" (p. 48) who viewed the development of communications technology as a means of solving most major social and economic problems. Another group included "professional futurists and writers and journalists," many of whom were staff writers and editors for major newspapers and monthly magazines. Individuals such as Kevin Kelly, John Perry Barlow, John Brockman, R. U. Sirius, and Rheingold himself were active participants in this community. In the next decade, this group and others who shared their views would become a source for a political orientation that took hold in the 1990s. That orientation is the new libertarianism.

New libertarians share a vision of a future in which new communication technologies will evolve to a state unimagined by those of us who do not follow computer science and cyberpunk fiction. As noted in the Introduction, this imagined future includes development of artificial intelligence (i.e., teaching computers to act intelligently) to the point where it exceeds human intelligence (Kurzweil, 1999). If the mind can be modeled so that its workings are better understood, one might eventually be able to store one's memory in a computer. One aspect of this vision is the desire to achieve immortality through disembodied intelligence. Another aspect is the hope that these downloaded minds could interact as a global consciousness, sharing experience and human wisdom on a planetary scale (Jordan, 1999).

New libertarianism is connected to political views endorsed by the Libertarian Party, which espouses reduction in corporate and personal taxes, deregulation of government, privatized health care, and free trade.[1] The party's view is that individuals in this new economy who are on the lower economic tier will benefit because they will share in the aggregate prosperity brought about by government deregulation and new technology (Hudson, 1997). For example, technological innovation could make school obsolete as students are released to work on their own, and the economy could regulate itself because currency traders and money managers would react spontaneously and as a group to economic conditions.

In the early 1990s, Louis Rossetto, a writer and editor who held this libertarian vision, returned to the United States from Amsterdam where he had been running *Electric Word*, a magazine concerned with information processing (Brockman, 1996). His plan was to start a new magazine that would help spread the new digital revolution to readers throughout the United States and the world. Eventually, he acquired funding from Nicholas Negroponte, head of MIT's media lab, and S. I. Newhouse, publishing magnate. In 1993, his company, Wired Ventures, Inc., was founded. The first product of the new company was the magazine, *Wired*, which sold 100,000 copies in its first issue and today has a circulation of over 500,000 (Fost, 1999; Goetz, 1997). Rossetto's vision developed into a multimedia enterprise, including Hardwired, a book publishing enterprise, and HotWired, which provided an online presence through an online magazine and a search engine. Rossetto's enterprises ex-

---

[1]For more information on libertarianism, consult the official Web site of the Libertarian Party at http://www.lp.org/ and in particular its "Issues and Positions" link.

panded too quickly, and he sold Wired Ventures in 1998 and left the company.[2] As this chapter shows, however, *Wired* continues to retain a number of writers who share the original vision (e.g., Kelly, Barlow, Negroponte, Esther Dyson, and Jaron Lanier), and the views articulated in its pages continue to be largely libertarian in nature and intent.

In an interview with David Hudson published in 1997, Rossetto explained what he viewed as the magazine's accomplishments. Its aim, he said, was to offer a unique, independent voice on the future of communications technology and to provide a venue for new ideas and discussion that transcend old politics and labels. The timing for the formation and genesis of *Wired* was right, he said, because the world stands on the cusp of massive social change due to new technologies, and forward thinking and innovation are called for. The magazine could help in this enterprise by providing intellectual leadership, as "the best ideas will win out because the universe does not reward inaccurate assessment of reality" (Hudson, 1997, p. 251). Because of its coverage of technology development, then, *Wired* could offer its readers the most recent and most accurate information about the new economy, product development, technology policy, and corporate enterprise.

Wired's approach to coverage of technology issues has been severely criticized by observers who believe that the magazine's writing is one-sided and propagandistic. In his article "The God of the Digerati," Purdy (1998) observed that "the picture of democracy that Wired honors rests not so much on shared deliberation as on spontaneous order," and that "Wired is redolent of intellectual pretense and factual delusion." Calling the magazine "the adolescent effusion of overgrown boys with too much money," Purdy noted at the same time that *Wired* is a "defining cultural document [that] demands attention." In *Educom Review*, Winner (1995) was even more harsh, criticizing *Wired*'s "fawning reports about hackers, computer entrepreneurs, media moguls,

---

[2]For more details on the history of *Wired*, see Simons (1996), Maloney (1998), Moran (1998), and Hudes (1998).

and cyberspace savants," and claiming that "almost without exception, the magazine prints only the sentiments of true believers, those convinced a digital civilization will inevitably be
superior to anything that came before."

Wired magazine has historically provided a venue for the discourse of the technological elite—computer scientists, new
product developers, telecommunications executives, and senior executives of major technology firms. With a subscriber
base of over one-half million, it serves as an important forum
for coverage of technology development and policy.[3] This
chapter uses rhetorical critical analysis to clarify how Wired's
content is designed for its reading audience. In particular, I examine how features of narrative structure in its articles (use of
time, portrayal of character, and use of culturally embedded
myth) promote libertarian values. By examining Wired's texts,
this chapter also discusses how metaphors and argument forms
include some clusters of shared community-based values and
exclude alternative values. In reading Wired from a rhetorical
perspective, this chapter complements other ideologically sensitive studies of Wired's writing (Millar, 1998; Schlosser-Hall,
1996) and examines how these features of its writing are designed to appeal to its readers.

One further contribution of this chapter is to show how
rhetorical patterns in a publication's content can change over
time. When Wired began in 1993, the Internet population was
overwhelmingly White, male, affluent, and technosavvy. By
2000, Internet users were much more diverse—equally balanced in gender and with broader involvement by minorities
and less affluent groups (Harris Interactive, 1999; Nua Ltd.,

---

[3]I selected Wired for analysis because of its significant role, historically and to date, as a
general circulation magazine for the technically savvy reader. Since its inception in 1993, it
has been the only continuously published monthly magazine in the United States that focuses on computers and society. This sets it apart from trade and industry publications such
as Information Week and Infoworld that focus on a narrower readership. Its broad appeal was
one reason that it was purchased by Condé Nast Publications. It currently ranks fourth
among their magazines in advertising activity behind Bride's, Vogue Teen, and The New Yorker,
and ahead of 11 other general interest periodicals they publish ("Group Publishers," 2001).

2000). Furthermore, the magazine's editorial board and writing staff have changed under new ownership. Study of the language and narrative patterns in its more recent articles indicates the magazine's changing identity. Many of its texts, graphics, photographs, and covers appear designed to appeal to its original readership, but other aspects of its content seem directed at a more diverse set of readers. Rhetorical analysis of *Wired*'s content thus shows how its potential for functioning as a public forum for discussion of major technology issues may be impeded by content that favors certain social groups and excludes other groups who might be interested in technological issues and policy.

NEW LIBERTARIANISM: THE IDEOLOGY OF *WIRED*

On its current home page, *Wired* describes itself as a periodical that "delivers incisive analysis and resonant storytelling from some of the world's most provocative writers" ("About Us," 1999). From this description, one might expect to find in the pages of *Wired* a penetrating examination of the issues related to computer technology and society. Rossetto, *Wired*'s former executive editor, said that the magazine's goal is to "report accurately on the future that's arriving" and "on the world that is really out there" (Hudson, 1997, p. 236). Rossetto further insisted that "discussion is the essence of democracy," that "there is no serious discussion of real issues in traditional public spaces" (p. 242), and that the Internet is one place that this can happen. It would seem to follow from this that, for informed discussion to take place, participants should be informed of all sides of pertinent issues. However, in Rossetto's view, this seemed not to be the case. Elsewhere in the same interview, he said that "the question is no longer what statists we should be supporting—republicans or democrats, communists or fascists. The question really is what sort of libertarians we should be supporting" (p. 239). It would seem that

Rossetto's concept of open discussion is noticeably weighted in favor of one point of view.

Some critics might describe the rhetoric of some libertarian writers as propaganda, but I would not go so far as to apply such a label to *Wired*. Instead, I would describe most of its writing as epideictic discourse. Epideictic is one of three genres of rhetoric originally described by Aristotle (G. Kennedy, 1991). Whereas deliberative rhetoric concerns itself primarily with what is advisable or advantageous in the future and judicial discourse is used to consider the past (as in the courts), epideictic rhetoric is ceremonial. G. Kennedy (1963) described the features of epideictic discourse in some detail. First, it concerns itself with topics that are considered to be uncontroversial; it is assumed that the audience already agrees with the speaker's values. Second, it has a formulaic quality, making use of patterns and arguments familiar to the audience. Third, it is viewed as performance; the speaker has succeeded when the audience comes to admire his or her presentation. Fourth, its aim is to reinforce and emphasize shared values rather than to stimulate critical thinking and deliberation. In other words, this form of speech is entertainment and not deliberation. Of this genre, G. Kennedy (1963) concluded that "being in no fear of contradiction, the speaker readily converts into universal values, if not eternal truths, that which has acquired a certain standing in the community" (Kennedy, 1963, p. 51).

This chapter illustrates many ways in which *Wired*'s writing is purely epideictic in character, possessing all of the attributes of epideictic discourse identified by G. Kennedy (1963). Its ceremonial nature is reflected in a tendency to celebrate new technology products, entrepreneurs, and businesses. It seems devoted to "speech in praise of" technology gurus who are to be viewed as role models by its reading audience. Its articles develop predictably, making use of recognizable, repetitive writing formulas. Its hypermediated, unconventional graphic presentation is highly performative and seemingly designed to evoke admiration rather than critical thought.

As I indicate later, *Wired* does on occasion publish articles critical of new communication technologies, but they are deviations from its norm. Because of its market niche and the support of advertisers selling new technology products, the magazine's editors and authors write for the digital generation of 20- to 30-somethings vested in technological innovation and entrepreneurship. As Schlosser-Hall (1996) noted in a study of the magazine, "political discourse in *Wired* magazine plugs into a historical narrative to constitute a subject position, the digital generation, and orients this implied audience toward political commitments" (p. 2). The magazine hails its readership as people who already share libertarian values. Thus, technological progress is often assumed to be inevitable, most readily developed through unregulated markets, and a major engine of economic growth.

Wired's identity is shaped by the tacit ideology of its originators and current editors and writers. This ideology is a major force in the magazine's design, coverage, tone, and message. The new libertarianism that pervades *Wired* places its faith in business investment, democratic egalitarianism, personal creativity, and economic growth. It abjures government regulation, social welfare, and limitations on free speech. This value system gives rise to four beliefs that go largely unquestioned in *Wired*'s articles and that, taken as a group, are highly compatible with libertarianism.

The first belief is that capitalist enterprise (rather than regulation or bureaucracy) can by itself solve all significant social problems. In the 1999 *Wired* article described in the Introduction, for example, Kelly (1999) explained how the problems of poverty, environmental degradation, and illiteracy could be solved through the economic growth engendered by new technologies. He predicted an uninterrupted period of ultraprosperity in the 21st century, a stock market that will hit 100,000 by 2025, mushrooming philanthropy, and a cleaned-up environment. In light of such prosperity and wealth, regulation and social welfare would seem unnecessary.

The second belief is that concerns about the digital divide will be addressed if everyone gets out of the way and allows innovation and entrepreneurship to take their course. Libertarians believe that economic growth benefits the poor through trickle-down prosperity. Likewise, today's technological innovation, introduced by a vanguard, will become tomorrow's commonplace as technology's tools and procedures become accessible to a larger number of users. This process was described by Jane Metcalf, president and cofounder of Wired Ventures, in a 1995 interview:

> There will be these jags of technology, when a new thing that only engineers can use is designed and then filters down through an interface-design process until it becomes accessible to a larger public. Meanwhile, the pioneers are out developing the next edition of the latest technology, which will be difficult to use and therefore inaccessible to the bulk of Web users. (Brockman, 1996, p. 225)

The idea, then, is to support innovation and new product development with the expectation that it will benefit everyone in the long run.

Third, there is a faith in the superiority of democratic systems accompanied by the idea that it is our obligation, "as citizens of a progressive nation, to provide inhabitants of less fortunate countries with the social, economic, and technological resources they need in order to succeed in the same ways that Americans have done" (Selfe, 1999, pp. 118–119). The belief that the comparatively less regulated economy of the United States fosters technological growth and innovation was made explicit by Rossetto when he said:

> The true measure of the failure of European (in other words, statist) direction of technology can be measured by the fact that in ten years, during the biggest technology boom the planet has ever witnessed, Europe has gone from a net exporter of technology to a net importer. (Rossetto, n.d.)

Wired's writers frequently make disparaging remarks about the backwardness of other countries. For example, Vietnam's state repression of the Internet was criticized (Case, 1997), as was Bulgaria's reliance on the black market (Bennahum, 1997).

France's dependence on Minitel was ridiculed (Lazarus, 1997), and China was described as having "a very bad government" (Sterling, 1998, p. 162). So the pattern goes.

Fourth, there is the consensus that humankind's future will be one of enhanced quality of life and shared consciousness, and computerization will make that possible. Wired's writers' preoccupation with artificial intelligence and emulating the function of the human brain is tied to the hope that, at some point in the not-too-distant future, a person's memory can be downloaded into a computer and he or she can live on after the demise of the body (Heron, 1998). Prior to that, there are said to be possibilities for unlimited connectivity among peoples everywhere, or, as Rossetto described it, "a global consciousness formed out of the discussions and negotiations and feelings shared by individuals connected to networks through brain appliances like computers. The more minds that connect, the more powerful the consciousness will be" (Hudson, 1997, p. 241). The New Libertarians of Wired, then, see technology as very possibly the way to immortality and shared consciousness in the future.

Readers and writers of Wired share a high level of consensus on such values as financial security, personal freedom, community, and creativity. They also share a common vision—a utopian future in which general economic prosperity benefits everyone and we all enjoy personal freedom and community in a clean environment where everyone prospers. Wired has been and is a celebration of these values and this vision. Thus, even as much of its writing deals with the future (normally the purview of deliberative discourse), its treatment of that future is, for most of its readers, largely uncontroversial.

This epideictic discourse is enacted in a number of ways. Articles in Wired are highly choreographed, making use of a pattern familiar to and enjoyed by readers. Most of these articles contain speech in praise of the young entrepreneur (or the successful executive who used to be a young entrepreneur). The use of narrative patterns and models is enhanced through associative and dissociative arguments and stylistic devices such as analogy, metaphor, personification, and double hierarchy. Furthermore, Wired's social Darwinist inclinations can be viewed through its absences: what is not discussed, who is not described, and the ways minority group members are treated when they are included at all. The remainder of this chapter discusses each of these features to reveal the rhetorical workings of *Wired*.

THE WRITING FORMULA: A SET PIECE

In his discussion of epideictic speech, G. Kennedy (1963) noted that in epideictic speaking and writing, the general organization and topics to be covered are so patterned and predictable that the speech assumes a ritual form. To sustain audience attention and allow space for virtuosity in its design, epideictic tolerates "some individual variation to give an illusion of novelty" (p. 154). In the epideictic of ancient Greece, Kennedy noted, the pattern was praise, lament, consolation.

There is a clear pattern, too, in most of the celebratory articles in *Wired*. (Many of the major essays are celebratory, but there are other kinds, such as descriptions of new technology, parodies, and political discussions of issues like encryption and free speech.) The celebratory articles begin by describing a situation; then they introduce a challenge, praise the entrepreneur who serves as a central figure, explain how his mind works, describe his plans for meeting the challenge, and conclude with the promise of his eventual success. Sometimes the order of the elements varies through the use of flashbacks, but the pattern itself remains highly recognizable.[4]

This pattern can be succinctly described by means of a sample essay—"One Huge Computer"—written by frequent contributor Kevin Kelly and his co-author, Spencer Reiss (1998). As the title implies, this article deals with product development on a device that would enable hardware connectivity and compatibility—"the network that makes all networks one, a global ner-

---

[4]For just a few examples, see E. I. Schwartz (1997), Wolf (1998), Bayers (1998), Frauenfelder (1999), and Kirsner (1999).

vous system" (p. 130). After a short orientation, the essay describes the setting:

> In a windowless second-floor room in a deliberately obscure Sun Microsystems outpost in Sunnyvale, California, half a dozen anonymous chunks of expensive-looking hardware sit on long folding tables. Some barely rate a first look: a not particularly recent printer, what looks like a pair of flat screen monitors, a video camera, a couple of keyboards. Turn any of the devices around, however, and only two wires are visible: electric power and an RJ-45 Ethernet connection. Each box ... is a fully independent network citizen, able to hold its own on the system, unencumbered by specialized cables, software drivers, or the rest of the usual array of digital life support. (p. 130)

This description of the situation also introduces the challenge, which is lack of uniformity and compatibility in the platforms that are linked into networks. This situation leads to hardware obsolescence, high requirements for intensive system maintenance, and other expensive and inconvenient outcomes.

One of the men working on this problem is Bill Joy. In recognition of his project's whimsical name, Jini (loosely mimicking the Arabic for magician), Joy is portrayed on the issue's cover as a genie. He is introduced quickly as someone who has

> made a second career out of keeping most of the Rocky Mountains between himself and the Silicon Valley. A founder of Sun Microsystems and still officially Sun's VP for research, Joy took himself to Aspen a decade ago to build a geek-lord's dream: his own custom research-and-development lab. (Kelly & Reiss, 1998, p. 132)

A picture of Joy's vision of the future is conveyed through an interview with him that accompanies the article. Joy clearly favors parsimony, compatibility, capacity development, and ease of use. He finds current programs such as Microsoft Windows NT compendious and unnecessarily complex. He seeks to anticipate and plan for a future in which present technologies will come up short because of inadequacies in their design.

The remainder of the article discusses various hardware and software products in development that are designed to meet this problem. In the end, the focus returns to Bill Joy and his work on Jini, a platform that enables all sorts of devices to work together on a network. The lines of competition are drawn (and this is the big picture): "NT's 20 million lines of code versus the 600 Kbytes of Jini. Bill versus Bill. Redmond versus Aspen" (Kelly & Reiss, 1998, p. 170). The authors' conclusion is optimistic because this solution is so needed and because Bill Joy is on the right track.

This pattern and its configuration of narrative elements have a powerful aesthetic appeal. Because habitual readers know the basic moves, they can fully appreciate the variations. In "One Huge Computer," the elements are out of sequence: The situation and challenge are introduced first, then the focus moves to Bill Joy through a sort of flashback. Suspense is introduced throughout when competing plans for meeting the challenge are discussed. However, everything turns out just fine in the end with the promise of "a global network so complex it will be a kind of organism, a dynamic, richly connected medium wrapped around the earth 24,000 miles deep" (Kelly & Reiss, 1988, p. 171).[5] The pleasure of reading a narrative of this sort arises in part from its predictability and in part because it coincides with the experiences of its readers. As a life script, Joy's story is representative "of actual stories the [reading] subject can take up and hold as constitutive of his personal identity" (Ricoeur, 1983/1984, p. 74). In Joy's challenges, struggles, and successes, readers can see their own.

The pages of Wired are filled with similar narratives of young people with desire and ambition. Typically, they focus on a central figure (usually male), and they praise entrepreneurship and capitalist enterprise. Even though the magazine was sold in 1998 to Condé Nast publications, the characters, plots, and outcomes of these narratives have remained essentially the same.

---

[5]Kelly and Reiss (1998) noted that the statement cited here was taken from the annual report from Daimler-Benz North America.

They provide a terministic screen—an instance of symbolic action that shapes perception and experience—through which readers can view their own personal experience (Burke, 1966). These narratives have a certain comforting, foreordained quality, because the entrepreneurs whose lives they narrate are always viewed as successful or potentially successful. The qualities of these narratives can be more fully laid out through an extended example of the personal experiences of a group of young hopefuls described in a 1999 issue of *Wired*.

The July cover that year featured a photograph (head shot) of five individuals—four young aspirants to success in the wired world, and the author who wrote about them, Po Bronson. The article in question, "GenEquity" (Bronson, 1999) tells the story of the four, along with two others who are not pictured. Bronson followed movements and developments in the lives of these six newcomers to the Silicon Valley. All six came with goals and dreams; what happened to them in the months following their arrival? Bronson's account is chronological, following these Gen-Xers' ups and downs as they tried to negotiate and succeed in the business environment they encountered. He intersperses their individual accounts during the summer and fall as he meets up with each of them from time to time. His narrative is quite gripping and most readers would read through to the end to find out what happened to each of these young people.

Bronson's article is of interest because of its importance (a cover story), length (21 pages of the issue), and general conformity to the ideology and type of writing characteristic of the magazine. It begins by portraying the Valley as a mecca, a land of opportunity in the classic American sense. One can nearly visualize the starry-eyed new arrivals in the opening paragraph:

> They come for the tremendous opportunity, believing that in no other place in the world right now can one person accomplish so much with talent, initiative, and a good idea. It's a region where who-you-know and how-much-money-you-have have never been less relevant to success. They come because it doesn't matter that they're young, or left college without a degree, or have dark skin,

or speak with an accent. They come even if it's illegal to come.
They come because they feel they'll regret it the rest of their lives if
they don't at least give it a try. They come to be a part of history, to
build the technology that will reshape how people will live 5 or 10
years from now. (Bronson, 1999, p. 113)

A sympathetic reading of this opening paragraph might hold that
Bronson wrote it this way simply to portray what the new arrivals ostensibly believe, because his own subsequent account im-
mediately makes it clear that many of these beliefs are false. In
the Valley, success depends very much on how well connected
one is, particularly to venture capitalists, banks, and lawyers.
Judgments are based readily on the number of degrees one holds,
who one knows, and one's work history. Nonetheless, beginning
the piece with "the American dream" makes for a good story. Because the advocacy of certain values and the purveyance of *Wired*
ideology in Bronson's article are very much tied in with the stories of the featured individuals, those stories must be retold here.

Thierry Levy has flown in from Paris for an Internet Show-
case in San Diego. He botches his presentation, but in contemplating his next move, decides to stay in the United States. He
cancels his flight back to France and goes to San Francisco instead. After driving around the Valley for a while, he settles into
a motel and contemplates his prospects. He has 70 days until his
passport expires. When Bronson looks him up 4 months later,
he has just rented an office and is preparing to market his product, Quiz Studio, a drag-and-drop tool for Web developers.
With an MBA from a prestigious French business school, a
promising product, and some French backers, he figures he can
make it. After all, as he reminds Bronson, his father, who had
been in the French resistance, always told him that America "is
the Place where Heroes Are From" (Bronson, 1999, p. 114).
Levy works 14-hour days, works out at the gym, and lives an as-
cetic lifestyle. In subsequent visits with Levy, Bronson finds
him progressively lonelier, more discouraged, and less enthusiastic about the United States. Even on the brink of bankruptcy,
however, Levy does not give up, and keeps his coders working
to get the bugs out of his software. At the end of Bronson's ac-

count, Levy's backers come through with another $150,000, giving him 6 more months to pull off the sale of his product.

Michael Zilly (a pseudonym) has come west from Massachusetts with his product SuperNova, a highly portable touch-screen technology, in tow. He developed this product with proceeds from the sale of illegal drugs that he raised in the swamps of western Massachusetts. To succeed in his venture, he needs to raise $80,000 in 3 months. Despite his degrees (a BS, an MBA, and part of an MS), he lacks class, dressing as a catalog shopper and speaking some sort of cultural hodgepodge. Zilly has many misadventures, making deals with a beltway bandit lender back east and working for a man whose company was indicted on 27 counts of fraud. In the end, Zilly, who is desperate for work, takes a COBOL class and works as a temp on Y2K projects for $35 per hour. The story ends well, however, when Zilly procures permanent employment at a major Valley computer firm.

Julie Blaustein, the only woman of the six people featured, has moved from Boston. Unlike the men, she has no entrepreneurial ambitions and few technical skills. Rather, her talents are in sales. Having made connections through her personal interest in Ultimate Frisbee, she gets many interviews but no job offers. (Bronson speculates that this is due to her weird speech pattern—a combination of Boston accent and Valley girl speech.) Finally, she procures a position with CitySearch and must make cold calls to sell the Chinese businesses in her assigned area on the idea of employing CitySearch to design Web sites for them. Her sales are low, and she becomes discouraged. Because she already has a "job hopper" profile, she feels she has few options. Her ambition is to work for Yahoo! and move to the city. After a few months, Julie is offered a position at a higher commission with GeoCities and accepts it. Fortunately for her, GeoCities is subsequently sold to Yahoo! so she is able to realize her ambition.

John/David Foster prefers to be called David even though his name is John because "there were too many Johns at his last job" (Bronson, 1999, p. 116). Unlike the other men in the story, he does not hold a college degree. He arrives in Silicon Valley from Salt Lake City, where he worked for a firm called ICentral

that "wasn't fun to be a part of anymore" (p. 116). He has gotten
a similar sales position in the Valley at a $21,000 salary, which
he is foregoing in lieu of a deal with his employer that, if he can
raise $500,000, he will receive a $100,000 salary. His employer,
eFree, is run by a 23-year-old boss who is paying only John/Da-
vid's living expenses. Shortly after John/David arrives in the
Valley, his old Salt Lake City firm is sold and it appears that if he
had remained with them, he would have made about $100,000.
John/David's faith in his new boss is soon shown to be misplaced, as his business fails, he does not pay John/David's rent
and bills, and John/David's possessions are in the hands of his
former landlord. Eventually, John/David has to sell his last possession, his car. At just about the same time, however, he starts
a new business as a consultant, offering business development
advice to small startups and established companies for a cut of
whatever deals he arranges. He quickly signs three customers,
hires a staff of eight, and remains optimistic, figuring he can
make it big with only one success.

Scott Krause comes from Tennessee with an MBA and a desire to "build the technology that changes how the world lives
and works" (Bronson, 1999, p. 119). Bronson is amazed by
Krause's sustained ebullient enthusiasm. Even though Krause
begins working for Infoseek and says he is working on a project
with "historic implications," that project is killed in the beta
phase. Krause is reassigned to a new project that would go online in 6 months to a year. He notes that in the meantime,
Infoseek stock has climbed from 16 to a high of 90, and he tells
Bronson, "When I was back in Tennessee ... I was so ready to
come out here. I dreamed of it, but I never thought that dream
would actually come true" (p. 179).

The sixth and most interesting case is that of Ben Chiu. A Taiwanese man who grew up in Toronto, Chiu is a 27-year-old former proprietor of karaoke clubs in Taiwan. He left Taiwan
because he was tired of having to "pay off" the right people to
stay in business. He has developed KillerApp, a price comparison shopping machine that finds the cheapest price for goods.
He works an 18-hour day and has no friends. In subsequent en-

counters with Chiu, Bronson realizes that Chiu is on the verge of success. At first, Chiu says he "can't talk about" what is going on (which means he's in negotiations). The next time Bronson talks with Chiu, nothing has happened but Chiu says that the window is still open to further developments. Eventually Chiu is connected up with mergers-and-acquisitions bankers and sells his KillerApp for more than $50 million, making more than $23 million on the deal. After signing the agreement though, Chiu has no one to celebrate with.

When thinking of these people's lives and how they are portrayed in Bronson's (1999) article, one can fully appreciate the extent to which much of the rhetoric of *Wired* is embedded in its narratives. These narratives can be considered in terms of what they emphasize, what they assume, and what they neglect or omit. Further, the narratives can be read as arguments from model in that they serve as a key to what is to be admired, provide patterns of behavior that are to be emulated, and, as such, encourage imitation (Perelman & Olbrechts-Tyteca, 1969). By considering the features of these narratives, one can discern the ideologies and values that they perpetuate in story form.

Levy, Zilly, Blaustein, Foster, Krause, and Chiu all appear to be seeking to establish an identity and lead better lives. In large part, they believe that money is the sign of success and that by succeeding they will make a mark and establish an identity for themselves. Levy notes that in the Silicon Valley, "the only value is system is money" (Bronson, 1999, p. 122). Money, however, is only a means to other ends. Bronson noted that "valley money … doesn't always seek out the highest return.… It's greedy sure, but it has all sorts of peripheral motives" (p. 172). In this view of value, the ultimate measure of a company is monetary—its revenues, its potential value in a public offering, and the likelihood that it might gain in value through merger and acquisition. Further, the measure of the individual is monetary. Until one has achieved financial success, his or her identity is unstable and insecure. The need to assign Michael Zilly a pseudonym shows him to be a shadow figure inhabiting the margins of Valley work and society.

John/David's name switch (emphasized throughout the article by use of the slash) signals that he is trying to discard an old Salt Lake City identity and reach for a new one. Ben Chiu seems to have a Taiwanese last name combined with an Anglicized first name. Blaustein and Zilly also struggle with identity issues on other fronts. Blaustein's inability to find a job is attributed to her Boston accent, and Zilly's "catalog-shopper's" attire reflects his liminal state. Once these people have made it in the Valley, they will presumably secure identities and styles suited to their environment.

The keys to success appear to be singlemindedness and asceticism. Levy inhabits a spartan office, works 14-hour days, and exercises at the gym. When Bronson goes to see him after a few months, he finds out that "he's off food entirely. He's switched over to the Apex nutritional system, powdered substances laced with amino acids.... Thierry still has no friends, no social life" (Bronson, 1999, p. 175). John/David chooses to forego his salary entirely and works for his company just for living expenses, primarily the rent on his studio apartment. Bronson noted that John/David has "eaten pancakes for dinner four nights straight" (p. 116). And, as noted, Chiu is so committed to work that he has no friends with whom to celebrate when he does achieve success. It is clear that none of this group thinks much about his or her fellow humans, service to society, formation and maintenance of friendships, or anything other than development of the product. The single exception appears to be Blaustein, who goes to the public library to mentor a child who needs help with reading and writing. If the others can spare any time for a social conscience, Bronson did not tell us about it.

Another point of emphasis belies the disclaimer Bronson made at the beginning of the essay: It is not what you know, it is who you know. By way of Levy, Bronson cited a commonly known statistic: Of every 1,000 business plans sent to venture capitalists, only 6 are accepted. All of the wanna-bes in the story do try to network with others: Blaustein with her frisbee friends, Levy with French executives, Zilly with workers at his computer company, and Chiu with Taiwanese investors. Of-

ten, a breakthrough comes when the individual is put in contact
with certain lawyers, bankers, and investors through intermediaries. Chiu, who left Taiwan to escape being beholden to such
intermediaries, finds that nothing is different in the Valley. To
be acquired, he concludes, one needs "name-brand VCs [ven-
ture capitalists]—well-connected investors.... It's guanxi all
over again" (Bronson, 1999, pp. 174–175). *Guanxi* is a Taiwanese term for connections.

Important dimensions of prevailing values emerge, too, in
what is omitted in the essay. There are many indications of questionable ethics on the part of these role models, but little commentary on them. Bronson (1999) reported that Levy obtained
an extension on his visa by masquerading as his own employer
back in France. John/David worked for a company that served
pornography site businesses. Zilly got started by raising and selling drugs, then sought backing from individuals with questionable criminal records. Chiu participated in a system of payoffs in
Taiwan to stay in business there. Evidently, such practices are
viewed as justified because they are what one must do to get
started and to survive in the business world. It could also be that
some readers of the essay would regard such practices as smart
and cool—ways to survive in an already corrupt world.

Another form of absence is exemplified in Bronson's han-
dling of Julie Blaustein. Her story receives comparatively less
space than the others, and Bronson devoted disproportionate
attention to her appearance. He described her as having "a
buxom bombshell figure, big auburn hair, high cheekbones,
and almond hooded eyes, though she is a sort of Cubist render-
ing of herself. One eye is higher than the other; a tooth is gray"
(Bronson, 1999, p. 168). Blaustein is one of only two subjects in
the article who is not an entrepreneur. She describes herself as
nontechnical; no mention is made of her education, and there is
only a passing mention of her work experience. The sexism of
Wired has been commented on by many observers and even ad-
mitted by its editors. At one point, Paulina Borsook (1996), a
disgruntled former writer for the magazine, counted how
many men and women were authors of stories, subjects of fea-

tures, or listed on the mastheads of the issues through 1995. She concluded that only 15% of *Wired* authors were women, women were the subject of about 15% of the articles, and women were shown on only 1 cover out of 25 as of June 1995. When Katrina Heron replaced Kevin Kelly as editor-in-chief, one might have hoped that things would improve, but only 2 of the 30 contributing writers listed in the July 1999 issue were women. In any case, Bronson's gendered characterization of Blaustein seems to be rather cavalier.

The narrative patterns and values reflected in Bronson's (1999) profiles of the young hopefuls can be found time and again in other personal stories and corporate development narratives in *Wired*. Like Bronson's characters, many of the entrepreneurs and CEOs treated in the magazine are described as driven, committed workaholics whose success is due to self-denial and singlemindedness. One interesting feature in many of their stories is connected to the roles of time and transcendence (Ricoeur, 1983/1984). Time is often viewed as inexorable—always running out. The central figure's passport will expire, or his money will run out, or he will no longer be able to find backers for product development. Narrated time in the stories unfolds in light of future time. The story is either told through "snapshot" interviews of central figures across time or through a combination of flashbacks viewed in light of forward-moving events.

These patterns of narrative and character portrayal, then, play very neatly into the mythos of technology development and the economic version of U.S. manifest destiny described in the Introduction. Berland (2000) referred to this pattern as "techno-evolutionism" and noted that it "relies on the assumption that human culture, democracy, freedom, and intelligence must and will progress along with our technology" (p. 243). She observed that "this is the secret of the technological utopic: technology both signifies and guarantees that change can only go forward, never backward" (p. 243). Successful futures seem foreordained in the narrative sequencing and flashbacks that structure the stories of most of the individuals in "GenEquity." These young arrivals to the Silicon Valley (including one European and one Taiwanese) believe that venture capitalism, free markets, and individual efforts are the key to success and freedom, and that the United States, and especially the Valley as its technological mecca, is the best site for their work. Furthermore, entrepreneurship, tireless work, and singlemindedness will reward their efforts in the short or long term.

There is also a sense of progressive refinement across time—in the products, speech, dress, and self-presentation of the central figures. Does their self-imposed asceticism—denial of friends, food, relaxation, and pleasure—represent some self-mortification in the hope of eventual transcendence? Are setbacks to be viewed as definitive, or only as waystations on the path to some glorious outcome? Evidently, they are only momentary. For example, at the darkest hour for all six of his characters, Bronson (1999) observed, "Nobody gave up. Nobody went home. Everyone's appetite had only been whetted" (p. 177). This persistent and inextinguishable optimism aligns with *Wired*'s epideictic mission. If the idea is to exhort the faithful and celebrate technology's bright future, a tragic outcome would be inappropriate. Only through a sustained focus on entrepreneurial success can libertarianism's bright future be realized.

ASSOCIATION AND DISSOCIATION— "STYLE" AS A FORM OF ARGUMENT

One of the features that draws readers to *Wired* is its style. With its lively parodies, narrativized reporting, vivid colors and simulations, frequent hyperbole, and upbeat attitude, the magazine is rarely boring. Along with the formulaic template that organizes elements in its essays, certain stylistic patterns occur frequently. These patterns are not only stylistic; they also perform an argumentative function.

Argumentation theorists Perelman and Olbrechts-Tyteca (1969) referred to such patterns as being associative and dissociative. They noted that the principal aim of many speakers and writers is to get their audiences to accept certain ideas and theses. One way to do this is to present thoughts and information in a way that encourages listeners and readers to reason in some particular way. Association and dissociation of ideas

enable this to happen. Association "brings separate items together and establishes a unity among them" (p. 190). This unifi-
cation encourages readers to relate ideas to each other through
some sort of liaison or link. Dissociation breaks a concept into
two ideas, assigning a higher value to one as opposed to the
other. Perelman and Olbrechts-Tyteca noted that associative
and dissociative processes are complementary and can be
readily viewed in terms of one another.

Associative arguments take many forms, such as argument
from cause, sign, or authority. In this section, I am particularly
concerned, however, with those forms of association that mark
Wired's writing. These include figurative analogy, metaphor,
and argument from model. These forms seem particularly ame-
nable to communicating the tacit ideology that underlies the
magazine's reportage.

Figurative analogies bring together two ideas, making the
less familiar of the two more understandable and accepted by
comparing it with the one that is more familiar. Perelman and
Olbrechts-Tyteca (1969) called the more familiar idea the *phoros*
and the less familiar the *theme*. By emphasizing aspects of each
of the two elements, the writer highlights those and neglects
other aspects. Comparisons made by figurative analogies are
relatively explicit. For example, one of *Wired*'s writers said:

> There are some [people] who have not been exposed to the re-
> wards of being an entrepreneur and don't know what they're miss-
> ing. But they're starting to hear about it, and they're getting antsy
> for a taste of it. It is as if they were sitting on the other side of a
> one-way mirror, watching people make love and wanting to be a
> part of it. (Platt, 1999, p. 129)

Implied here is that, if the experience of entrepreneurship is like
making love, it involves concentration, withholding, excitement,
and culmination in a "rush." Male readers of *Wired* would probably get a vivid idea of the attractions of entrepreneurship from this
comparison. Another figurative analogy supports the brain–computer connection discussed earlier: "Like another well-known dis-
tributed computing device—the human brain—[the global

network structure] will need to be able endlessly to reconfigure itself, to solve unanticipated problems, and address unforeseeable
new needs" (Kelly & Reiss, 1998, p. 130). Here the global network
structure is anthropomorphized through the attribution of the human capacity to adapt, anticipate, improvise, and resolve.
Anthropomorphizing computers, computer systems, and other
technologies is a regular feature of Wired's writing.

  Although it appears more stylistic than argumentative, metaphor is another association playing a vital role in furthering the
Wired mind-set. Metaphors are collapsed analogies in which conceptual fusion can be effected in a single word. One metaphorical
cluster in Wired is that of "the race." For example, as one CEO in-
terviewed for an essay observed, "When you're faced with a dis-
ruptive new technology, you've got to recognize its implications
more quickly or—like the dinosaur—you'll watch the mammals
eat your eggs" (Bayers, 1998, p. 168). In many write-ups about
product development and corporate decision making, writers
imply that the first person or company to the market with a new
idea or product will succeed. Making the most of one's opportunities is therefore essential. Vital to this is the ability to anticipate
future developments and take risks based on one's judgments.

  Another metaphorical cluster is that of contagion. Contagions
are usually viewed as spreading quickly, inexorably, and uncon-
trollably. This metaphorical cluster gains potency through its
tacit association with computer viruses. Most of Wired's readership has had the experience of being unknowingly zapped by
computer viruses and losing work time and money as a result.
Aligning any phenomenon with a fast-spreading virus implies
certain inevitable outcomes. After noting the spread of electronic
devices in his own home, Kelly concluded that "technology is an
active virus trying out all possible shapes and functions. It will try
out anything. It continues to shrink to invisibility in chips and expand to gargantuan scales in cities. And once present, technology
rarely retreats" ("The wired diaries," 1998, p. 134). As noted earlier, Wired constructs its readership as a group that views technological development as inevitable. The contagion cluster
contributes to this idea, therefore short-circuiting deliberation

about technology and its effects. As Berland (2000) noted, the inevitability of technological development absolves writers and their readers of any need for empirical analysis or for public research and debate.

A third type of associational element is argument from model. As I have noted, in *Wired*'s case, the model to be emulated is the young entrepreneur. Nearly all of these individuals are White men under 30.[6] The entrepreneur is the personification of libertarian ideology. Most of them are viewed as brilliant, focused, and farsighted. They are geeks or former geeks who know how computers work and are technologically astute. Behind their imposing public face, most of them are portrayed as basically nice guys. Nevertheless, most of them are also fearless and often are feared.

Perelman and Olbrechts-Tyteca (1969) noted that arguments from model function to regulate behavior and focus on the specific case. They also provide a basis for identity formation on the part of readers, implying the roles they see themselves playing, the traits to which they aspire, and success in an environment where one's place in the social hierarchy is judged through success. *Wired*'s encomia to various entrepreneurs fit in nicely with its epideictic mission—speech in praise of the individual and his or her accomplishments.

Associational arguments, then, conceive of technology development as an inevitable, vital process, and they encourage readers to be involved in the business and social scene related to it. Whereas associations explicitly reveal what is to be valued by the reading audience, dissociations form value pairs and are thus very revealing of what is devalued. Close study of patterns of dissociated ideas in which one element—affluence, technical knowledge, success—is systematically valued over opposing elements can reveal much about writers' underlying ideology. Consider, for example, the following statement: "Goldbart contends that the suddenly wealthy, not the envious have-nots,

---

[6]For an accounting of gender balance in *Wired*'s coverage, see the next section of this chapter.

are at risk these days" (It's a bitch, 1999, p. 76). This dissociation separates those who are newcomers to wealth from those who have not succeeded; but it does more than that: It assigns a special status to the "suddenly wealthy," that of being "at risk." Perelman and Olbrechts-Tyteca (1969) would write this as a double hierarchy, with the more valued member of the pair serving as the "denominator" of a conceptualized pair:

Have-nots	Not at risk
Suddenly wealthy	At risk

As shown here and in the next chapter, the devalued "numerators" of these value pairs are prototypically descriptive of technological have-nots, Luddites, women, minorities, and other groups who do not make up *Wired*'s readership. *Wired*'s marginalization of these groups becomes clear through these absences. Because dissociations expose the devalued poles that serve as foils to what is explicitly advocated, they are useful in revealing what is systematically excluded or marginalized in a text.

What dissociative patterns does one find in *Wired*? Empirical study of dissociation shows that it occurs less frequently than other forms of argument, but its impact is often more noticeable (Warnick & Kline, 1992). Therefore, the dissociations that we do find should be noted with some care. Furthermore, the dissociations occurring in *Wired*'s features and essays exhibit some recurring patterns and threads that are of interest. The magazine's practice of habitually celebrating technological expertise, innovation, and new products is reflected not only in its narratives and writing formulae, but also in recurrent patterns of dissociation.

Most of *Wired*'s contributors subscribe to the idea that the advent of personal computing and the Internet marks a watershed in communications technology. Rejection of the inevitable infusion of new technologies into our lives and work is therefore viewed as either quaint or misguided. For example,

Negroponte (1998) reminded his readers that "people concerned about tomorrow just cannot settle for the tools of yesterday" (p. 184), and Bill Gates, Sr. insisted that "the Internet and distance learning is almost certainly a more effective way of teaching than what we've been doing" (Johns, 1999, p. 149). These dissociations place whatever is "new" in the preferred position:

Old	Tools of yesterday	[Traditional teaching]
New	Tools of tomorrow	Internet and distance learning

Another set of dissociations clusters around technological expertise. They are complemented by a sort of nostalgia associated with the pre-Windows, pre-graphical user interface (GUI) days that ended in the 1980s. In those days, people knew code, assembled their own computers, and built their own applications. An example of this orientation can be seen in Bennahum's (1998) "When We Were Young," where the author reminisced about the days when, as a student, he mastered programming. Now, he noted, "we're supposed to know how to use the tools, not make the tools" (p. 129). Programmers and hackers who know the code share the mystery, along with the students in Bennahum's classroom who "were not covering well worn paths but striking out, sometimes wildly, into little known territory" (p. 190). These dissociations can be displayed as follows:

Knowing how to use the tools	Covering well-worn paths
Knowing how to make the tools	Striking out into new territory

This special access to knowledge inaccessible to the rest of us makes its bearers seem special, somehow smarter and better than everyone else.

Dissociations are frequently used to remodel audiences' views of reality. A new ideology such as libertarianism can become established through reinforcement of value pairs such as old–new, unskilled–technically astute, hesitant–forceful, and conservative–bold. Dissociations, along with associations that seem on their face to be "merely" stylistic, support and reinforce the values and views embedded in the larger narratives of entrepreneurship and innovation that are repeated so frequently in *Wired*'s pages that they come to seem like mantra. This tendency hardly promotes critical thinking on the part of the magazine's readership, partly because, as Perelman and Olbrechts-Tyteca (1969) observed, "once the concepts have been dissociated and restructured, [the effect tends] to react on the aggregate of concepts into which it is inserted" (p. 415).

RACE, GENDER, AND *WIRED*

The phenomena of absence and devaluation that appear in certain of the dissociated value pairs discussed in the preceding section can also be seen in other ways. *Wired*'s articles narrate the lives its readers would like to live; its value pairs reinforce the hierarchies to which readers already subscribe. In light of this, we might also expect that the proportionate coverage and portrayal of women and minority groups in *Wired* would reflect this same marginalization and devaluation. The problem with absence, neglect, and negative stereotyping is that minority readers cannot see themselves in the pages of *Wired*; if they are uninvolved with and ambivalent about new technologies, *Wired* would contribute nothing to change that situation.

An apologist for *Wired* might say that its patterns of coverage merely reflect the demographics of its readership and of the online population in general. After all, in the early days of the World Wide Web (when *Wired* was founded and developed its initial subscriber base), the Internet was largely populated by affluent White men. Castells (1996) cited a 1995 report that estimated that 67% of Internet users were male, more than half were aged 18 to 24, and their median household income was between $50,000 and $75,000 (Lohr, 1995). Three years later, more than half of first-time Internet users were female, 72%

were over 30, and 46% made less than $50,000 (Pew Research Center for People and the Press, 1998).

The Internet has clearly become more diverse, as the percentage of adults using it has grown from 9% in 1995 to 56% in 1999 (Harris Interactive, 1999). A 1999 Harris poll indicated that, whereas 76% of all adults were White, 81% of those online at that time were White; whereas 12% of adults were African American, 7% of online users were African American; and whereas 10% of adults were Hispanic, 9% of online users were Hispanic (Harris Interactive, 1999).

If the Internet population and potential subscribers to *Wired* have come to look more and more like the general adult population, then one might anticipate that its coverage of technological issues would change. One might expect it to include a larger proportion of new products, media outlets, entrepreneurs, and business leaders who would attract the interest of women, minorities, and middle-class citizens. What this section of the chapter shows is that, although the demographics of its editorial board have changed and its range of topics has broadened, *Wired*'s reportage is still noticeably tilted toward the interests and prejudices of technosavvy White male readers.

One way to examine *Wired* to see whether its content is skewed toward the White men is simply to tabulate the amount of coverage allotted to various groups. A second way is to consider how non-Whites and women appear in *Wired*'s writing and photographs. Are they exoticized, demeaned, or positioned differently than White men? If these practices do occur, are they infrequent or are they a pattern? The remainder of this section uses these two methods, among others, to explore treatment of race and gender in the magazine's pages.

To arrive at a quantitative estimate of coverage, I counted the numbers of various groups in pictures accompanying articles. I excluded the cover, title pages, advertisements, cartoons, drawings, and simulations.[7] My count included five issues over

---

[7] I also excluded background figures who were too small to see clearly.

a 5-year span (1995–1999): 3.09, 5.09, 6.08, 7.06, and 7.09. The tally is shown in Table 1.1.

A simple count, however, does not reveal the whole picture, and a closer look at the photographs and accompanying commentary shows many of the portrayals of women and minorities to be marginalizing or unflattering. Of the 15 Asian men, 2 were pictured as convenience store clerks in 7.09 (p. 105), and 12 were displayed as primitives carrying a house by hand in 6.08 (p. 105). Portrayals of women include Sandy Lerner in 7.09, who is noted for her tendency to donate money to fund searches for extraterrestrials. Martha Stewart, in the article "I Do Have a Brain," commented on the aesthetics of computers as home decoration in 6.08. Donna Rice Hughes, who is pictured as digitally blindfolded in 6.08, is unflatteringly described as an antipornography campaigner. Furthermore, most of the write-ups of women in these issues were asides, consuming one page or less of layout.

Concerned about this apparent pattern, I decided to pursue a more qualitative approach and surveyed *Wired*'s coverage of

TABLE 1.1

Sample of Groups Represented in Wired Magazine

Group	n	%
White men	194	71%
White women	40	14.7%
African American men	10	5%
African American women	2	>1%
Asian men	15	5.5%
Asian women	1	>1%
Latina women	1	>1%
Uncertain	9	1.3%
Totals	272	99.5+%

women and ethnic groups in 9 other issues from 1998 and 1999.[8] Here, the same frequency patterns seemed to occur, but the nature of the portrayals was either neutral or favorable. Of 12 women, 2 were lawyers, 1 was an executive, 3 were designers, 1 was a musician, 1 was a salesperson, 1 was a rock climber, and 1 was a broker or liaison. A negative portrayal of a "cybercensor" was balanced with a favorable one of a free-speech advocate. Women were still shortchanged on space, with the longest of these articles being two pages and most running less than a page. Non-White women included one Latina, a business advisor, and one Iraqi architect.

The differences between portrayals of women in these issues and Asian and Asian American men were noticeable. Whereas women were often featured for their artistic or creative ability, Asian men were viewed as technologically astute businessmen. Two were CEOs; three were involved in product development and business startups, one was in sales, and one was a prime minister. Among Asian women, one was a political leader, one a vice president of marketing, and one a graduate student. An Asian American family of four was pictured in a photo essay spoof as customers of Fry's Electronics. These issues included features on only two African American men and two Hispanic men (there were no women in either group). Anecdotally, I can say that there appeared to be a much better race balance in the magazine's advertisements than in its coverage. It also appeared that in both sets of magazine issues, coverage of women and minority groups was more a sidebar than the focus of attention.

Wired's libertarianism also comes through in the treatment of race by its authors and writers. Although there was very little explicit discussion of race as an issue, certain viewpoints were tolerated and published that reveal a political agenda. For example, in the "Gen Equity" essay, Bronson (1999) explained Julie Blaustein's difficulties finding employment by noting that "if you're white and educated, it's fair to hold all sorts of preju-

---

[8]I used the same procedures I described for my first survey, except that I did not include White men. Issues included were 6.04, 05, 06, 07, 10, 11, 12, and 7.06 and 09.

dices against you" (p. 168). Whites, in other words, are (as we know) victims of reverse discrimination. When queried about his views on government and politics, idealab!'s Bill Gross fantasized about how to optimally organize a society:

> How you organize the physical structure, to optimize where businesses are located, where homes are located, traffic flow, things like that. And I've also thought how you could *screen the people you let into the country, so that they share similar intellectual values*. (Platt, 1999b, p. 132, italics added)

That such a homogenized designer society might seem attractive to *Wired*'s readers reveals something significant about their attitudes and values.

Whereas White male entrepreneurs and CEOs are described in a manner that borders on adulation, African Americans do not fare as well. In an article on a hip-hop music firm, Felicia Palmer, the firm's marketer, is described as a woman whose "mouth works fine—all the time" (Freund, 1997, p. 197). The writer seems amazed that her business partner, Pascal Antoine (who, incidentally, attended MIT and worked in its media lab) "speaks in grammatically correct sentences at all times" (p. 198). In another article on a budding Web development business in Bedford Stuyvesent, *Wired*'s writer seemed obsessed with the venue, titling the article "Roaches in the Machine" and leading off with a description of the "roach defogged apartment" in which the business was sited (Mays, 1997). It is not uncommon, then, for the behavior and appearance of the non-White men and the women who appear in the magazine's pages to be described as unattractive, inappropriate, or unpleasant. Treatment such as this reveals insensitivity, or at least indifference, to issues of race.

The pattern of indifference to race was also evident in Katz's (1995) article, "Guilty," in the September 1995 issue of *Wired*. The issue's cover featured a whitened, Arnold Schwarzeneggerized, digitally altered picture of O. J. Simpson and next to it the moniker Guilty. Objectivity is obsolete." What would this cover lead the reader to infer about the essay's position and argument? Inside, the photo is of a blackened Nicole Simpson and a whitened O. J. Is the article about race issues in America? No, it is rather an indictment of journalism and journalists' failure to cover "the enormous social, ethnic, and political changes" permeating the culture as shown in the trial proceedings (Katz, 1995, p. 130). Katz also criticized the bickering, posturing, and maneuvering in the trial, and he concluded that the justice system is unduly influenced by money, media coverage, and racial divisions.

Race is an inconvenient fact for technophile prophets such as Kelly, Negroponte, and Katz, who prefer to believe that the presence of technology and new media will help to equalize the United States. Although there is gradually increasing minority participation in Internet activity, it is also pretty apparent that online venues will not be freer of hierarchy, marginalization, racism, or exclusivity than is "meatspace." The Net is made up, after all, of people, and people do not radically change their values and attitudes when they come online. The ways that *Wired* handles issues of race, or rather fails to handle them, pretending instead that they do not exist, is itself an example of the blindness of "Whiteness" to issues of race in U.S. society (Nakayama & Krizek, 1995).

THE NEW *WIRED*: A CHANGE IN CHARACTER?

The preceding sections of this chapter dealt with the profile and character of *Wired* during the first 6 years of its publication. Under the direction of Louis Rossetto and his team of writers, the magazine was designed by and for the technological elite—the computer culture of the developing Internet and the World Wide Web. In light of the changing Internet population and *Wired*'s new ownership, however, I felt it would be desirable to reconsider its content in late 1999 and 2000. Although the staff of editors and writers continued to be predominantly male, new writers had joined the magazine over the 2 years after it was acquired by Condé Nast. The list of contributing writers still retained some of the same names as in 1998, including Barlow, Dyson, Lanier, and Negroponte, but their contributions were infrequent, and *Wired* appeared to be using more freelance material. Could it be that the character of *Wired* had changed to include a wider range of viewpoints and appeals to a broader set of interests?

The answer to this question appeared to be mixed. A survey of the magazine's content in 1999 and early 2000 showed the same patterns of epideictic writing, optimistic prognostication, and celebration of free market capitalism that had marked earlier issues. There were, however, occasional deviations from this norm, and in one feature article a strong warning about future catastrophes that could result from unthinking, rapid development of new technologies such as robotics, genetic engineering, and nanotechnology. This new tendency to tell both sides of the story means that *Wired* could become a platform and venue for deliberation about technology development, especially if the magazine's coverage becomes more balanced.

To reassess *Wired*'s potential role in this area, I read all of five recent issues—October, November, and December 1999 and January and February 2000—plus additional articles in later 2000. Although it continued to focus largely on new computer technology, *Wired* also broadened its scope to include new genres such as fiction (e.g., Sterling, 2000) and new topics such as technology more broadly conceived. For example, there were articles on container shipping in 7.10 (Taggart, 1999), avant-garde musical instruments in 7.11 (Lehman, 1999), and Japan's culture of "cute" in 7.12 (Roach, 1999).

Overall, the topics of the 56 features and sidebars fell into three major categories—technology development (28.6%), individual technoachievement (30.4%), and general interest (33.9%). Articles in the first category, technology development, were inclined to herald new technologies or new development in existing technologies. Their focus was primarily on the technology itself and only incidentally on the people who developed it. Articles in this category included a series on microcinema and use of digital video to film movies cheaply in 7.10 (Kenner, 1999; Parks, 1999b), digiscents (computer-generated scents) in 7.11 (Platt, 1999c), and the emerging chip technology of magical microbots in 8.01 (Leonard, 2000).

These articles concentrated on explaining the new technology, describing product development to date, and predicting its use in the future. Technical difficulties that might impede or slow down implementation were discussed in passing, but risks and disadvantages were largely ignored. In some cases, there were testaments to the idea that "the future is already here," as when Kenner (1999) on microcinema claimed that "suddenly the cinematic landscape is changing.... Hollywood moguls are finding themselves playing catch up to digital billionaires in the power game" (p. 217). Future predictions about potential new technology applications were also quite bold, as in Leonard's (2000) view of microelectromechanical systems:

> MEMs will soon be ubiquitous. There will be the far out (airborne micro flying machines, networked minibots) and the practical (disposable blood pressure gauges, wearable pollution sensors).... As these sensors and actuators ... permeate the world, the fabric of daily existence will come alive. (p. 162).

This unbridled confidence in the nature and effects of future technology development enables readers to envision radical change and dramatic improvements in convenience and the quality of life. Although such predictions may entertain and inform, they are unlikely to provoke critical thought or examination of potential economic, environmental, or social effects of these technologies.

The second category—individual technoachievement—included 17 of the 56 feature articles. This type of article, which dominated the magazine in *Wired*'s early years, has now been joined by other genres, but it remains a staple of the magazine's content. It can be distinguished from features with a technology focus by its emphasis on the accomplishments of a single individual or a group. Its elements include the person or group as visionary, belief in self and eventual success, overcoming of adversity, risk taking, self-denial, and successful execution of the technological vision.

In Sheff's (1999) account of "Sony's Plan for World Recreation," for example, Sony's decision to shift to new media technologies such as robotics, home networks, and ubiquitous computing is told through accounts of work by its management team to innovate in a corporate environment resistant to change. In "Code Warrior," Bayers (1999) offered a detailed description of Microsoft's Jim Allchin and his difficult role in developing Windows NT. In "The 38-Gigahertz Breakthrough," Platt (1999a) depicts efforts to build a broadband network of wireless dish antennae on the roofs of New York skyscrapers. These antennae play a key role in maintaining high-capacity connectivity among Win Star clients in metropolitan areas. The man responsible for this breakthrough is Bill Rouhana, who correctly predicted the eventual success of wireless as a cheaper, easier way of providing connectivity. A fourth example of this genre is Kirsner's (2000) description of Martin Nisenholtz's efforts to found and develop the electronic version of *The New York Times*.

This article contains all the crucial elements of articles featuring accomplishments of individual entrepreneurs and managers. It begins by tracking Nisenholtz's physical movement between *Times* headquarters and his office across Times Square at Times Company Digital. This account of his daily shuttling metaphorically represents his continual efforts to bridge the staid edifice of respected old media with the irreverent, innovative practices of new media news. By means of an abbreviated biography, the writer revealed Nisenholtz's vision, prescience, and belief in himself. He reported that "Nisenholtz demonstrated a fascination with media early on and has experimented with various versions of it throughout his career" (Kirsner, 2000, p. 126). From his early experiments with photography and amateur filmmaking to use of primitive videotex and low-resolution computer graphics, Nisenholtz showed himself to be a new media visionary, described by co-workers as able to predict "things that were going to happen on the media scene before any of us even knew about them" (p. 132). Despite others' disregard, their tendency to "belittle and make fun of" him, and their apathy and indifference, Nisenholtz persevered.

Hired by the *Times* in 1995 to create digital services for the newspaper, Nisenholtz drummed up support, bided his time, designed a revenue-generating business model, negotiated a deal with the Newspaper Guild, developed and retained employees, and, at the time of the *Wired* essay, was readying the digital division for an initial public offering (IPO). In the interim, he evidently rejected many offers of more lucrative employment, believing that what he could accomplish at the *Times* was more meaningful. In the end, the article concludes, "a successful IPO will likely make him a multimillionaire—but more succinctly, will win him back credit of all those years of pushing water uphill" (Kirsner, 2000, p. 142). Nisenholtz thus models all the characteristics that breed success—vision, brilliance, persistence, self-sacrifice, and personal strength.

The articles in this genre reprise much of the writing in *Wired's* early years. Their preoccupation with personal achievement, financial success, technological innovation, and wealth may inspire readers who can see themselves in such stories, but these stories are unlikely to deal with larger issues. Recent articles in the third category of general interest (e.g., history of computing, new forms of architecture, presidential campaign, medical technology) may have informed readers, but only rarely raised issues concerning ethics of new technology innovation.

In its coverage of ethnic groups and foreign cultures, *Wired's* content seems to be becoming more balanced, perhaps reflecting the globalization of the Internet and increasing participation in computer culture in the United States by ethnic groups and women. In the five issues I used to reconsider *Wired's* more recent coverage, there was generally more attention to positive portrayals of these groups. The article on DigiScent in 7.11, for example, provided very favorable images of two African American executives of a firm developing a computer-generated odor synthesizer (Platt, 1999c). Another general interest feature focused on efforts by Chinese in China and Chinese abroad to develop Sina.com—a "Chinese AOL" linking Chinese from around the world (Sheff, 1999).

Wired's tendency to stigmatize or exoticize such groups has hardly disappeared, however. The December 1999 cover featured an anonymous, naked African American woman jumping off a cliff with the comment "Here we go … " (clearly a reference to its being the last issue of the old millennium). This cover inspired the following comment from a reader:

> Until now, Wired has never displayed a black woman prominently on its cover. Congratulations! Not only is she black, she's naked and jumping off a cliff. That's certainly in the spirit of your two covers featuring black men. They've both been criminals: O. J. Simpson (*Wired* 3.03) and a cracker (*Wired* 2.12). I'm sure this is all just unconscious creativity. But that's the problem: unconsciousness! (Edwards, 2000, p. 69)

Other issues in this time period included features on spam generated by a supposed African American con man (Parks, 1999a), the backwardness of Cambodia (Leslie, 1999), and the wackiness of Japan's culture of "cute" (Roach, 1999). Racial and ethnic balance in *Wired* may be forthcoming, but it is not yet present.

A detailed textual reading of the ways in which *Wired*'s writers make use of narrative, style, argument, and imagery, then, tells us a good deal about its presumed readers, their beliefs and values, and the libertarian views that they hold. In regard to time, the narrative time in *Wired* is nearly always viewed as future oriented, as running out, as progressing toward some unknown yet known outcome. Its central characters are generally viewed as heroes of a sort whose ingenuity, resourcefulness, asceticism, and diligence are to be envied. In *Wired*'s language use, metaphor and dissociation systematically give presence and immediacy to value clusters concentrating on individualism, personal freedom, technological innovation, and wealth. Either through implication or explicit disparagement, other values are passed over or rejected. These expressive patterns, combined with stereotypes or exoticizations of women and racial minorities, reinforce social hierarchy and marginalization. The world envisioned by *Wired*'s writers and readers would be free of government regulation, infused by new technology, and isolated from poverty and disease. It would be a world where the technological elite survive and prosper, while everyone else benefits, as much as possible, from the trickle-down benefits of their work.

BILL JOY ON THE FUTURE: A SIGNAL EVENT

Wired's potential for serving as a platform for serious discussion of the ethics of technology development was unexpectedly and dramatically made clear in April 2000 when noted software developer and programmer Bill Joy wrote issue 8.04's featured article on the technology future. This essay was noteworthy for its placement (in *Wired* of all places), dire predictions (including possible destruction of the world and demise of the human race), and the credibility of its author (highly respected among the technological elite). Joy provided a clear, sober, realistic assessment of possible future developments in robotics, genetics, and nanotechnology, and his aim was clearly to sound a warning and attract media attention to his message.[9]

Joy began by ruminating on Kurzweil's (1999) predictions that artificial intelligence will exceed human intelligence and that humans will become one with robotic technology. Although Joy (2000) took Kurzweil's predictions seriously, he said, "I felt sure he had to be understating the dangers, understating the bad outcome along his path" (p. 239). The unease caused by this realization set Joy on a course of inquiry to discover worst case scenarios that could occur if the ethics of technology development remain unexamined.

Joy then reviewed past technologies that have created frightening new problems because of unintended consequences. These include antibiotic-resistant bacteria and malarial parasites with drug-resistant genes. Joy also described the develop-

---

[9]For other examples of articles reporting on the downside of technology, see Paulsen (1998), Ogilvy (1998), Kirsner (1999), and Rheingold (1999).

ment of the atom bomb and the uncontrollable arms race that ensued. In recounting how and why the bombs were dropped on Hiroshima and then Nagasaki, Joy (2000) reminded readers of the later statement by physicist Freeman Dyson that "the reason it was dropped was just that *nobody had the courage or foresight to say no*" (p. 250, italics added).

On Joy's account, we have good reason to be concerned about 21st century technology development. Genetics, robotics, and nanotechnologies all have the capacity to be self-replicating—to reproduce themselves. When we have designed intelligent robots, Joy (2000) observed, "it is only a small step to a robot species"—a species that can produce copies of itself (p. 244). As Haraway (1997) showed us, we are already on the way to cyborgization of humans through microcomputers, implants, and other devices. The question of when human becomes nonhuman and whether nonhuman will replace the human has become much less futuristic than it used to be. And, as Joy (2000) noted, "genetic engineering technology is already very far along" (p. 244). We consume genetically modified foods and we have cloned animals. One possible outcome of this was imagined by Joy: If we can reengineer ourselves into unequal species (perhaps creating a superrace), what would happen to humanity?

Nanotechnology—manipulation of matter at the microlevel—caused Joy (2000) even greater concern. Creating new forms of animal and plant life is very risky, particularly because "it is far easier to create destructive uses for nanotechnology than constructive ones" (p. 246). Joy believed it entirely possible that self-replicating life forms could run amuck, destroying the environment and crowding out other life forms. He concluded that "we run a grave risk—the risk that we might destroy the biosphere on which all life depends" (p. 246).

Joy also emphasized commercial interests' disincentive to publicize or discuss these risks. The genetics, nanotechnology, and robotics technologies (GNRs) are enormously profitable, and there is no profit in publicizing their dangers. In contrast to large-scale

20th-century technologies developed largely in government laboratories, GNRs are being developed by corporations. As Joy (2000) noted, "In this age of triumphant commercialism, technology—with science as its handmaiden—is delivering a series of almost magical inventions that are the most phenomenally lucrative ever seen" (p. 248). There is a great deal to be gained monetarily from their development and little return on reminding the public of their risks.

Joy (2000) concluded his discussion by contemplating measures that could be taken to forestall and perhaps eliminate the social and environmental risks engendered by GNRs. The first and most prominent of these is relinquishment—foregoing research and development of new technologies with risks that we cannot now predict. The model for this, Joy argued, is the unilateral U.S. abandonment of biological weapons development. Recognizing the possibility that such technology could fall into terrorist hands, the U.S. government agreed to the 1972 Biological Weapons Convention and the 1993 Chemical Weapons Convention. Joy acknowledged the difficulties of verifying relinquishment by other parties, but he argued that the problem of verification was not unsolvable.

Joy then called on scientists and engineers to adopt a code of ethics similar to the Hippocratic Oath that presumably would incorporate the commitment to do no harm and to whistleblow as necessary to forestall technology development that is potentially life threatening to humanity and to the earth. By explicitly describing the risks of GNRs, considering the means of addressing them, and, most important, describing ethical stances other than those giving the unquestioned presumption to technological development and free market capitalism as good in themselves, Joy's essay aimed to instigate discussion and controversy. He concluded by saying, "My immediate hope is to participate in a much larger discussion of the issues raised here, with people from many different backgrounds, in settings not predisposed to fear or favor technology for its own sake" (Joy, 2000, p. 262).

CONCLUSION

Subsequent media discussion of Joy's (2000) essay was substantial, and his work undoubtedly had the impact he had hoped for. In the months following appearance of Joy's essay, media coverage of his article included appearances on PBS, NPR, the BBC, Australian and Canadian television, innumerable Web sites, and in prominent newspapers (Allis, 2000). On April 1, 2000, a major symposium was held at Stanford University involving the following participants: Ray Kurzweil, inventor of the reading machine for the blind; John Holland, professor of computer science and psychology at the University of Michigan; Hans Moravec, pioneer of mobile robot research; Kevin Kelly, former editor of *Wired*; Ralph Merkle, computer scientist and researcher in nanotechnology; John Koza, inventor of genetic programming; and Bill Joy himself. The discussion revolved around the following questions, as listed in the announcement of the symposium:

> Where will emerging research areas such as artificial life, artificial intelligence, nanotechnology, and genetic programming (as well as other areas that have not yet been dreamt of) lead? Will thinking computers succeed us as the most intelligent beings? Will our children—or perhaps our grandchildren—be the last generation to experience "the human condition?" Will immortality take over from mortality? Will personalities blur and merge and interpenetrate as the need for biological bodies and brains recedes into the past? What is to come? (Symbolic Systems Program, 2000)

In discussing these possibilities, the panelists represented a range of viewpoints. For example, Kurzweil led off by emphasizing the very real possibility of reverse engineering the human brain so as to reproduce its function in silicon. Joy responded by warning of the threats caused by self-replicating technologies, and he again recommended restraint in technological development. Merkle (2000) called for more research and stronger theory rather than relinquishment, and he seemed to advocate a "wait and see" option.

These reactions resemble stances taken in the press and on Web sites in response to Joy's (2000) essay. An article in *The Boston Globe* noted that Joy's "credentials elevate his standing as a critic of our current social trajectory, and his writing has triggered a debate that is long overdue" (Allis, 2000). A *Washington Post* editorialist concluded that he could "not imagine that anyone went away from discussion [of the issues raised by Joy] without worrying in new ways about what Joy called 'this century of danger'—and wondering what to do about it" (Ignatius, 2000). Following this eruption of controversy about the effects of this triad of GNR techonologies on human life and society, one might agree with Allis's (2000) speculation that there has been a "conspiracy of silence" in technology coverage by media about these issues.

Essentially, this chapter has been concerned with that conspiracy of silence. It is not in the interests of *Wired*, the technological elite, the corporations who invest in technology, or members of the academy who do research in these areas to raise serious questions about whether such research and development ought to proceed. As a widely recognized periodical about the people, businesses, products, and practices involved in hardware and software development, *Wired* provides a potentially valuable platform for discussion of the future of technology and its relation to the welfare and interests of the human species. Its publication of Joy's (2000) long, thoughtful article makes it clear that *Wired* can influence the thinking of its influential readership in important ways. The appearance of Joy's piece also indicates that *Wired* is prepared to perform this function, but its owners, editorialists, and writers may to some extent need to rethink their preferences and priorities to do so.

They may need to invest less energy and space in applauding advances in biotechnology, artificial intelligence, and virtual reality and more in raising serious issues about their effects on people and society. The editorial stance of *Wired* could move away from its libertarian stance and its tendency to intensify and celebrate its readers' existing values. In the short term, such actions might seem to work against the magazine's existing interests. One observer noted that Joy's warning was all the more credible because it conflicted directly with his financial interest (Stross, 2000). The same is probably true of *Wired*, but it could be that greater breadth and inclusiveness in its coverage, pro and con, of new technology could make it a major force in the media landscape of the 21st century.

CHAPTER TWO

Masculinizing the Feminine:
Inviting Women Online ca. 1997

The December 1997 issue of *Wired* magazine reported a survey of 1,444 randomly selected Americans that was intended to explode some myths about public participation on the Internet (Katz, 1997). The survey divided its sample into four groups: the "superconnected," who use e-mail at least 3 days per week, plus a laptop, cell phone, beeper, and home computer; the "connected," who use e-mail at least 3 days per week, plus three of the four other technologies; the "semiconnected," who use at least one but not four of the technologies; and the "unconnected," who use none.

Leaving the semiconnected (62% of the sample) out of the picture, Katz (1997) proceeded to compare the technologically savvy superconnected and connected groups (labeled "Digital Citizens" and comprising 8.5% of the sample) with the technologically bereft unconnected (29% of the sample). He argued that those whose lives are technologically enhanced are poised to lead the political system, positive about the future, optimistic, and eager to embrace change. Sometimes explicitly and other times by implication, he noted that the unconnected are much less sanguine about the future. Furthermore, he noted, Digital Citizens are better educated (more than half being college graduates, compared with 16% of the unconnected) and more enlightened (79% favoring a diverse workforce, as compared with 49% of the unconnected) than the technologically deprived group. Late in the article, seemingly unaware of the ways in which the bipolarity and marginalization of his own writing may have influenced his readers, Katz demurred that "the tone of rhetoric coming from Digital Citizens ... has often been so shrouded in technobabble and arrogance that it has taken on an elitism of its own" (p. 274)

Katz's article serves as both a sign and an example for the analysis in this chapter. His essay is a sign of the elitism so prevalent in discourse about technology. Technophile rhetors often tacitly describe themselves as resourceful, knowledgeable, innovative, and in control, and their technophobic counterparts as fearful, ill-informed, regressive, and hesitant. This chapter focuses on one site of this elitism—discourse in books, trade periodicals, and gateway Web sites inviting women online during and prior to 1997.[1]

Katz's article serves as an example because he uses various rhetorical strategies that mark the discursive construction of elitism. These include argument from model, argument from hierarchy, dissociation, and metaphor. For example, his use of the term Digital Citizen (capitalized) invests this construct as a model that others should emulate. Selecting two groups—the unconnected versus the connected—and ignoring the semiconnected, Katz polarized the sample and set up a technophobe–technophile hierarchy. By ascribing the positive traits of optimism, confidence, vision, and engagement to the Digital Citizen, Katz (1997) dissociated this construct from the stereotype of the technie as isolated geek and made his argument that the connected are "a vast, well-educated political constituency that remains up for grabs" (p. 78). By applying such terms as "bellweather" (p. 68) and "vibrant community" (p. 78) to Digital Citizens, the article further invests this term with value for its readers.

Inspired by Turkle's (1995) observation that "we construct our technologies, and our technologies construct us and our times" (p. 46), this chapter considers how ideology is embedded in this invita-

---

[1]The period 1995 to 1997 was selected because it was during this time that female participation began to grow rapidly. The third annual Graphics, Visualization, and Usability Center survey of Web users (conducted April 10–May 10, 1995) reported female participation at 15.5% of users (Graphics, Visualization, and Usability Center, 1995); the eighth survey (conducted October 10–November 16, 1997) reported female participation at 38.5% (Graphics, Visualization, and Usability Center, 1997). In collecting articles and Web sites for this study, two research assistants and I searched general periodical indexes and book catalogs for articles and books inviting women online, and we accessed and surveyed top-ranked sites on Lycos, WWWomen, and other search engines.

tional discourse addressed to women in the mid-1990s. I consider how the presence and promise of new technologies might affect how women think about themselves and their relation to such technologies, and how elitist discourse excludes and marginalizes women even while it attempts to invite them online. The phenomenon I describe constitutes a type of appeal to women, but it is by no means the only discursive type to be found. Many books and Web sites intended for women, especially those recently or currently developed, exemplify a more inclusive approach. Indeed, I conclude the chapter by describing a range of women's Web sites, from commercialized, elitist sites to socially conscious and inclusive ones. Nevertheless, during the mid-1990s, the type of discourse I describe in the early portion of the chapter and its rhetorical features was fairly ubiquitous and continues to be critically of interest.

This chapter carries forward a research program called for by Gurak (1997) in her book-length study of public advocacy in the Lotus Marketplace and Clipper Chip controversies. She noted that "it is important to move away from generalizations about life in cyberspace and begin to analyze specific instances of computer-mediated communication, not only as a way of understanding patterns of current discourse but also as a method of building theory" (p. ix). As I have argued elsewhere (Warnick, 1998b), rhetorical critics can and should adapt their methods to the study of rhetoric in new communication environments. Whereas mass communications scholars and researchers in interpersonal, organizational, and small group communication have been studying computer-mediated communication (CMC) for some time, rhetorical critics are relatively new to the scene.[2] It has taken some time to muster critical resources devel-

---

[2]Mass communications research has been concerned, for example, with how First Amendment protections and intellectual and property rights transfer from print to CMC, what factors draw audiences to Internet sites, and what strategies can be used to determine the accuracy of information on the Internet. Interpersonal communication researchers have studied the development and maintenance of relationships online, and small group researchers have examined the dynamics of group process in computer-mediated environments. Book-length works discussing the rhetorical dimensions of CMC include Chesebro and Bonsell (1989), Doheny-Farina (1996), Gurak (1997), and Lanham (1993).

oped for the study of agent-centered, stable, unitary texts intended for identifiable audiences and to adapt them to the
criticism of texts that are often anonymous, dispersed, frag-
mented, and constructed for audiences whose reactions are
hard to identify and describe.

Nevertheless, as I have shown in chapter 1, it is possible to
adapt rhetorical critical methods to the study of computer-mediated discourse. This remains a discursive environment in which communicators support values and ideologies,
influence one another, and shape beliefs and attitudes. As this
chapter illustrates, the critic can discern how audiences are
hailed or interpellated, how metanarratives are constructed,
how style enhances message appeal, and how certain interests
are marginalized in CMC. This can be done by studying texts as
systems: noting recurrent patterns of appeal, construction of
ethos in texts, who can speak, who is silenced, and how identities are discursively constructed.

My work is informed by some of the recommendations for
critical praxis put forward by Fraser (1989). She called for an
open, pragmatic, holistic approach to the criticism of social texts,
one that distinguishes "between the frame of a social practice and
a move within it" and that "implies an appreciation of the way
background institutions and habits prestructure the foreground
possibilities available to individuals in social life" (p. 106). The
emphasis here is on the ways masculine gender constructions—aggressiveness, resourcefulness, opportunism, and technical proficiency—are highlighted in discourse designed to
appeal to women. This study also follows Fraser's interest in "the
decisive importance of language in political life" (p. 106), the way
it shapes identity, forms expectation, and structures experience.

This chapter notes the characteristics of 1995 to 1997 print media discourse urging women to go online, describes identities
touted in many of the early Web sites designed to appeal to
women, speculates on the significance of metanarratives embedded in this discourse, and concludes by describing the more recent inclusive and versatile sites for women, teens, and girls on
the Web. This chapter focuses on asynchronous one-to-many

discourse on Web sites and is intended to complement work done on gender constructions in Internet Relay Chat (Rodino, 1997), discussion lists (Herring, 1994), and electronic lists and newsgroups (Gurak, 1997).

HIERARCHICAL APPEALS IN INVITATIONAL DISCOURSE

From 1994 to 1997, the growth of the Internet was phenomenal and, even as it grew, the demographics of Internet use changed dramatically. Georgia Tech's Graphic, Visualization, and Usability Center tracked participation among Web users from January 1994 when there were around 1,250 Web servers and 95% of the user population was estimated to be male. Their 1997 survey, run from October 10 through November 16 of that year, estimated that there were over 1 million Web servers and that about 40% of the U.S. respondents were female. The survey noted that this proportion was surprising when compared with the previous three surveys that showed the proportion of females hovering consistently around 31% (Graphics, Visualization, and Usability Center, 1997). It appeared that something was happening on the Internet that led to a sudden increase in the level of female participation. As I hope to show, one of the reasons for this increased participation may have been that there was more available in this medium that was of interest to women than there had been previously.

Even as female participation grew, various vested interests sought to increase it still further. Recognizing that "women are typically the household shopper" and that they "have tremendous buying power" (Kantrowitz, 1994, p. 54), every sort of company from cosmetics firms to booksellers to entertainment franchisers advertised on women's Web sites. Advertisers' interest in developing Web-based markets for their products aligns with their interest in the female consumer. As Fraser (1989) observed, "the sexual division of domestic labor assigns to women the work—and it is indeed work though unpaid and usually unrecognized work—of purchasing and preparing goods and services for domestic consumption.... [Consumer goods] advertising has nearly always interpellated its subject, the consumer, as feminine" (p. 125).[3] In addition, marketers of the online services and paraphernalia required by new users have also joined forces to get women connected. Furthermore, many feminist and grass roots organizations seek to increase membership and monetary support through online appeals to women.

As Turkle (1984) showed in her extensive ethnographic work observing computer use, humans' awareness of their own thought and lives can be deeply and reciprocally influenced by their online and computer-mediated experiences. To take her observations one step further, we might want to contemplate the ways in which people's relationship to technology is itself a construction. This construction, which currently attracts intense interest in the media, shapes and perpetuates many aspects of gender identity. Is the computer-mediated environment that will come to dominate the next millennium going to be one in which women share some modicum of equality with men, or is it one in which their self-concept, interests, and aims will continue to be marginalized? Turkle (1995) wrote that there was "potential for a more welcoming environment for women, humanists and artists in the technical culture" (p. 63). But do we see this potential beginning to be actualized today? The answer to this question depends on where one looks for it. The invitational discourse described in the early portion of this chapter appeared to displace the interests and identities of the female audience, whereas the newly developed Web sites described later on presented a very different picture.

The critical narrative informing my examination of invitational discourse is inspired by Burke's (1996) observation that human beings are "goaded by the spirit of hierarchy" (pp.

---

[3]The sense of the term interpellate as used throughout this chapter is taken from Althusser (1972): "[A]ll ideology hails or interpellates concrete individuals as concrete subjects, by the functioning of the category of the subject" (p. 173). Althusser further noted that interpellating an individual mirrors the process in which a policeperson would say, "Hey, you there!" At the point that the hailed individual turns around, recognizing that he or she is the person hailed, he or she becomes a subject. In an excellent discussion of interpellation, Butler (1997) has explained how the subject who acknowledges the terms in which she is hailed is herself complicit in the process.

15–16). By this, Burke gave a form or structure to human action that implies that all humans are intrinsically motivated by the principle of perfection, the need to move upward (mostly, and sometimes downward) in the many hierarchies that shape their social, political, and spiritual lives. If Burke (1950) is also right that "the cult of commodities [is] a mode of transcendence" (p. 192), then the hierarchies that infuse our consciousness include being more "in the know" (initiated into the mystery), better endowed with resources, and more capable of acquiring more knowledge and resources than the next person.

Our consciousness is shaped by hierarchy because the hierarchic principle "is inevitable in systematic thought" and "indigenous to all well-rounded human thinking" (Burke, 1950, p. 141). In my view, Burke's emphasis on the inevitability and ubiquitousness of hierarchy provides valuable fodder for the rhetorical critic of public discourse. Hierarchies embed themselves in the constructs of gender, race, profession, religion, and personal interest. These hierarchies are infused with the mysteries of social order and social estrangement. Because as human beings we are hierarchically motivated and also intrinsically symbol using (symbol making, symbol misusing) animals (Burke, 1966), our symbolicity provides the means by which hierarchies are expressed, invoked, entrenched, and overcome. Rhetorically, we express hierarchy through both association and dissociation (Perelman & Olbrechts-Tyteca, 1969). Associative arguments bring together ideas and elements and organize or evaluate them positively or negatively in terms of one another. In so doing, they order values hierarchically in relation to each other and to the consciousness of the audience to whom the associations are expressed.

Associations take many forms. They are expressed in metaphors and analogies in which the phoros, or element known to the audience, is brought together with a theme, or lesser known element, and value is transferred between the two. In invitational discourse, the phoros will possess desirable qualities that attract the reader, or undesirable qualities to avoid, as, for example, in this statement: "People without access to technology will be like those at an earlier time who lacked access to books and literacy" (cited in Penn, 1997, p. 3). The transference of a negative value from the phoros (illiterates in the past) to the theme (the "unconnected" in the present) serves as a hierarchically motivating and persuasive appeal (Perelman & Olbrechts-Tyteca, 1969). Likewise, arguments from model and antimodel function in much the same way, touting desirable features or outcomes that accrue to the technologically advantaged individual or (in the case of antimodel) benefits of which the technologically disadvantaged or challenged individual would be deprived. Frequently in the discourses I describe here, particular instances of individual success are put forward as models and their positive features are emphasized. This gives presence and value to these instances, enhances them with social mystery, and presumably provides a goad to those readers who are hierarchically motivated.

However, enhancement of presence is not the only suasive device available in these appeals. They are particularly of interest in the absences that characterize them. How are the subjects to whom they are addressed interpellated or hailed? What tacit attributes are assigned to these subjects? Where do the unspoken value orderings implicit in these interpellations place their reader subjects in the social and economic hierarchies? One useful way for the rhetorical critic to answer such questions is through the study of dissociative arguments and value orderings implied but not explicitly stated.

As I noted in chapter 1, dissociations break down concepts into pairs, giving a higher value to one of the concepts and a lesser value to the other, as in the distinction between appearance and reality, which is the dissociative prototype (Perelman & Olbrechts-Tyteca, 1969). For example, one might say "the Internet is not an assemblage of computers but a global meeting of minds" (J. Schwartz, 1996, p. 52). Here the author dissociated community (reality) from technological apparatus (appearance) and placed value on the idea of community to appeal to readers. Dissociations are relatively infrequent but nevertheless significant when they are used because they reveal the underlying value pairs embedded in a text. For example, the occasional dissociations occurring in discourse inviting women online counterposed such valued terms as future, community, and creativity, to devalued terms such as past practice, anonymity, and isolation.

Most dissociations arise from value orderings that mark cultural consciousness and practice. In a survey of value pairs in Western society, for example, rhetorician Olbrechts-Tyteca (1979) took note of orderings such as means versus ends, subjective versus objective, and normal versus unique, with the latter (the end, the objective, the unique) being the valued terms of each pair. A presupposition of the method used in my study is that every time a rhetorical appeal reinforces hierarchy by positing a valued term, it tacitly devalues some other term to which it is opposed. The tacitly devalued, unspoken terms comprise through absence a picture of what is excluded or marginalized in the discourse.

Many appeals to nonparticipating women to come online between 1995 and 1997 valued activity, aggression, currency, technology and wealth, and they devalued their opposites—passivity, hesitancy, convention, and poverty. The hierarchically motivated and enacted appeals thus interpellated the women in their audience in ways that may have marginalized and excluded them at the same time that they ostensibly sought to invite and include them. This phenomenon probably had implications for the success of these appeals and for the public awareness of the online environment and how it operated.

CONVERTING THE UNINITIATED: APPEALS IN PRINT MEDIA

Just prior to 1997, many media pundits, journalists, and feminist researchers were explaining women's disinterest in the Internet by describing it as an environment hostile to women. Constructed by predominantly male programmers, inhabited by young men raised on Battle Zone computer games, and frequented by seekers of cyberporn, the Internet was viewed as an environment that had nothing to offer women.

The sheer size and seeming complexity of the Internet seemed to have a chilling effect on women's interest in venturing online. Playing off of the coined term *cyberspace* (Gibson, 1984), journalists and pundits described the Internet as a "a vast realm," a "seemingly borderless world," a "trackless forest," a "digital jungle" and a "bizarre universe."[4] This huge and unknown space was furthermore viewed as having "dark alleys and odd characters to avoid" (Sherman, 1995, p. 27). In April 1997, *Ms.* magazine described a lurid, sado-masochistic gang rape in an America Online chat room. The article's author concluded that "it is not that all, or even most, Internet sex is violent; rather, that the potential for violent intrusions hovers around any exchange, be it sexual or not" (Michals, 1997, p. 69). The author's report of two women who were assaulted and killed by men they met online was hardly reassuring. Fears engendered by reports such as this were only reinforced by other articles in the popular press reporting abduction, harassment, and intimidation of women participating in chat rooms. listservs, and bulletin board postings (Nicholas, 1995; Segell, 1997).

Despite such warnings, the Internet was also portrayed in the popular press as a place of opportunity, something women hesitant to venture online were missing out on. Described as "crowded, full of interesting people and places," and as a "new medium" and a "new culture" (Sherman, 1995, p. 27), the Internet was viewed as a venue of opportunity, a place "where free individuals come together to create a whole that is far larger than the sum of its parts" (Brame, 1996, p. 32). The Internet must have seemed to some readers to be a tantalizing place, a place of possibilities for developing one's professional and personal life. Women who had not ventured online were therefore getting mixed messages. Was the Net a place to be sought out or avoided? Was it a venue for self-development or a site of oppression and violence? Although some of the invitations in print media to women to come online provided a balanced analysis of the negative and positive aspects of the

---

[4]See Glassman (1995), Sherman (1995), J. Schwartz (1996), and Sinclair (1996).

Internet, many others were one-sided with the presence given exclusively either to risks or benefits of online participation.

Just as there are many kinds of women and female interests that could be attracted to the Internet, so is there a wide variety of messages that could be used to appeal to women to come online. The diversity of potential female Internet users was reflected in the diversity of Web sites that came online during this period. Carla Sinclair (1996), who did a survey of them for her book, *Net Chick*, observed, "by the time I finished, there were so many sites that I couldn't keep up" (Ladd, 1996, par. 21). Long-standing sites such as feminist discussion groups, the National Organization for Women's (NOW) Web page, and FeMiNa, were joined by sites on fashion, health news, travel, and entertainment targeted specifically to school-aged girls, teenagers, Gen-Xers, or stay-at-home moms. The variety of particular interests and potential audiences notwithstanding, appeals to take up the Internet can be grouped into genres, each of which has characteristics adapted to the exigencies of rhetorical context and potential readership interest.

A logical place to begin study of appeals to come online is in women's and general interest periodicals. Those interests seeking to persuade women to try the Internet attempted to reach the nonparticipants through print publications that appealed to the mass female audience. A review of these revealed such articles as "The Infinite Possibilities of Going Online" in *Cosmopolitan* (Glassman, 1995), "Claiming Cyberspace" in *Ms.* magazine (Sherman, 1995), and "The Web: A Complete Women's Guide" in *Glamour* (Thomas, 1997). Authors of such articles faced a number of rhetorical challenges, not the least of which was the need for an exigence. Bitzer (1968) described the rhetorical exigence as "an imperfection marked by urgency" or "something waiting to be done" (p. 6). Authors who would persuade women to come online were writing for an audience whose many members saw no need to do so. Many school-aged girls, for example, were not necessarily drawn to technology. They were reported to be as interested as boys in computers— until about the fifth grade, when sex-role socialization processes turned them away from technology along with math and science (Kantrowitz, 1994). Also, prior to 1997, computer games were oriented exclusively to boys, featuring war games, conflict, blood, death, and auto races. Aside from educational CD-ROMs and software, there was little of interest for girls (Beato, 1997).

Women, particularly women with families and children, may have felt that they had little reason to go online. Their reluctance may have been due to a lack of fiscal resources to acquire the necessary equipment and software. As Fraser (1989) reported, women as a group were significantly poorer than men and composed nearly two thirds of all U.S. adults below the official poverty line. Disproportionately, minorities and women do not have the discretionary income to afford entertainment and conveniences. S. E. Miller (1996) reported that statistics from a National Consumer Law Center study in Boston indicated that 27% of African American and Hispanic families and about 10% of White families with incomes under $10,000 could not afford basic telephone service in the 1990s. Add to this that new technologies outstrip old and render computer equipment obsolete within 3 years. Miller reported that standard PCs in 1995 were sold with 540-megabyte (MB) hard drives, 1.4-MB floppy disk drives, and 8 MB of random access memory (RAM). This standard seemed very inadequate 3 years later, with 32 MB of RAM required to adequately handle software and Web browsing. Given the shortage of resources and the requirements of technological development, the requirement to maintain a household computer system was beyond the reach of many. As Coralee Whitcomb (1996) of NOW observed, "for many adult women of today, access to computer and Internet literacy is simply out of their reach" (par. 5).

Fiscal difficulties aside, there is also the issue of time; the woman who works full time in a nontechnical field, maintains a home, and spends time with her children may have priorities other than surfing the Web. Adding to the disincentives to online interest was considerable skepticism about the benefits of CMC. "What's in it for me?" such women might ask. Authors of invitational articles were hard pressed to answer this question. Their efforts to create an exigence—both for their own rhetoric and for online participation—often seemed less than compelling.

To overcome female reluctance to experiment with online communication, invitational articles in the popular print media enacted a pattern of appeals. First, they described the benefits of Internet use; second, they provided role models of women who have prospered online; third, they tried to facilitate action by explaining the equipment and measures needed to get online; and fourth, they resorted to a sort of "just do it" approach. The last of these may have been off-putting if not marginalizing to many readers.

The benefits the articles posited for going online included meeting new people, building community with other women, improving job and career prospects, and supporting hobbies such as cooking, quilting, gardening, and media design. *Cosmopolitan* ran a special feature in its April 1996 issue about eight couples (women 24–39 years; men 25–40 years) who met online, then in person, then courted and, without exception, invariably married. With one exception, all the men were white-collar professionals and presumably well-heeled (Astor, 1996). Aliza Sherman, whose Web site, Cybergrrl Webstation is discussed later, described connections to other women and to women's issues: "Women and activists are now communicating on line through Virtual Sisterhood, an Internet mailing list where one of the current topics of discussion is the 1995 United Nations conference in Beijing. From this list alone, I have been introduced to women from all over North and South America, Europe, and Asia" (Sherman, 1995, p. 28).

Working Woman promised its readers that "there's a whole World Wide Web of information out there that can help you do your job, run your business, and build your career" (J. Schwartz, 1996, p. 49). To prove this point, the article described women such as Kim Polese, member of the Sun Microsystems team that developed Java, "a figurehead for insurgent software engineers yearning to breathe free" (Fryer, 1997, p. 36). Polese was described along with Caitlin Curtin, President and CEO of Luminaire, a San Francisco software firm whose sales exceeded

$6 million in 1994; Stacy Horn, Founder and President of Echo (East Coast Hang Out) Communications Group; and Sally Narodick, Chair and CEO of Edmark, an educational software company that made $31 million in 1995 (Schuyler & Barad, 1996). (All of the bios of these women emphasized company profits and monetary success.) Presumably, these and other women represented the wealth and career success to be had by women who become involved in careers in communications, technology, software development, and multimedia. *Glamour* promised its readers, "it won't be long before women will need on line skills to qualify even for low-tech positions"; women who master Web surfing now will "put themselves ahead of the job hunting pack" (Thomas, 1997, p. 248). J. Morgan (1995) reminded her African American readers in *Essence* that "in ten years telecommunications and the computer industries are going to comprise 20 percent of our gross national product. That means if we intend to compete in tomorrow's job market—or have our children compete—we had better get with the program" (par. 22).

So, to meet a new man in her life, network with other women, and embark on an exciting and profitable career, "all" a woman had to do was "get connected." For Web surfing, "all" that was normally required was a new computer with the necessary memory, color display, sound card and speakers that are "beefy enough to take advantage of the Web's rich color, sound, and video" (Thomas, 1997, p. 249). Oh, and there's the second phone line so that the user "won't miss phone calls when [she's] Web surfing" (p. 249), the mouse, the modem, the software, and, of course, the online account. Where could the underemployed working mom with kids to feed and educate and a mortgage to pay find the resources to acquire the hardware, software, and online infrastructure to support her cyberactivity? Easy: Do without something else! J. Morgan (1995) advised her middle-class African American readers to do without "those Air Jordans, those Steelers jackets and brand-new Beamers" (par. 24), along with one of the average African American family's two TV sets. Even sacrifices such as these, however, would not have paid half the cost of a setup such as that just described, which is the minimum required to load and read many of the animated Web sites then available. (Reading most of the new Webzines for women such as *Minx, Maxi, Bust, and gURL* in 1997 required at least 16 MB of RAM and a full-color display. Many sites cheerfully reminded the reader: "Can't read this menu? Upgrade your computer!")

The idea that all this might seem too intimidating—too personally and fiscally difficult—leads to the final tactic of these invitational articles, the "look, just do it" appeal. Such appeals are sparked by a sense of seeming urgency, as in Whitcomb's (1996) view that "the adult women of today, despite our generation's uneven start into the Information Age, cannot afford to wait. We must stake our claim to the Internet now" (par. 6). (One should note the tendency to work from the metaphor of a frontier that must be occupied.) Another article by Wertheim (1996) in *Glamour* reminded its readers, "You like money. You like power. So, why are you ignoring the skills you need to get them?" Wertheim concluded that "many women have not been taught to feel comfortable with technology; even more of us are simply apathetic about it. But it would be a tragedy if our progress in the workplace were halted by our own passivity" (p. 153). Sherman (1995) was even more unequivocal when she argued in *Ms.* magazine that "women need to throw out excuses and embrace technology, especially something as useful and far reaching as the Internet, otherwise we are the ones holding ourselves back from truly gaining power in this area" (p. 28).

Women, then, were doubly disempowered. Grappling with the homework of family care, frequently marginalized in the workplace, sexually harassed offline and potentially online as well, they themselves were supposed to take the blame for not being more technologically savvy. Certain authors held women responsible for missing out on the benefits to them and their families of the new technologies because of their own passivity and inaction. One way to think about this is in terms suggested by Stone (1995) in her book, *The War of Desire and Technology at the Close of the Mechanical Age:* "Entry into the world of virtual com-

munity requires high levels of skills in the English language and a
high level of technical proficiency.... Many researchers, some
quite naively, tend to see cyberspace as a space of possibility precisely because it can give the (facile) illusion of a level playing
field" (p. 181). Not only was the playing field not level, but
thoughtless invitations to "just do it" ignored the economic and
lifestyle realities of many women. Compared to the invitational
rhetoric of popular press authors that I just described, however,
the rhetoric of another group could be (depending on its audience) marginalizing in the extreme. Let us call this group the
"cybergrrls."

CYBERGRRL DISCOURSE ON THE WEB

Cybergrrls (self-named to distinguish themselves from the
"girls" of Internet pornography) became very active on the Net,
putting up Web sites to market their own media design activities and other products. Many cybergrrls used their sites partially to invite women online and get them involved in
Web-based activities. Their sites appeared to be directed at a
younger crowd of Gen-Xers and adolescent teens. Sherman
(1998), for example reported that visitors to her Cybergrrl
Webstation site included a 62% representation between 18 and
35 and 24% between 36 and 55 and that their median household
income was $58,000. The discourse addressed to this audience
was characterized by certain recognizable terms, metaphors,
and identities.

The cybergrrls producing this discourse have described
themselves variously as grrls, gURLS, and nerdgirls. Taking
their inspiration from the Riot Grrls' interest in alternative
bands of "snarling sassy rockers" (Sherman, 1997a, par. 3), and
postfeminist backlash against political correctness, these
women have established themselves on the Net with Web sites
like Sherman's Cybergrrl Webstation (www.cybergrrl.com),
Carla Sinclair's Net Chick (www.cyberorganic.com /Peo-
ple/carla/), and Rosie X's Geekgirl. I have already mentioned
Sherman (1997b), one of the principal spokeswomen of this

group, who described herself as "boldly going where no grrrl has gone before" (par. 3). She said of her early days with the computer that she would "look at the strange box and the ASCI text" and would want to "go inside and figure it all out ... without any training, manuals, or help" (Sherman, 1997b, par. 4). Describing Net women as "creative, innovative, and adventurous" (Sherman, in Sinclair, 1996, p. 86), Sherman said she was "flabbergasted" that more women were not going online. As noted in the preceding section, she was one of the touters of the "just do it" appeals.

Sherman and her colleagues were viewed by Kristin Spence, writer for *Wired*, as belonging to the vanguard of women (of which Spence counted herself a member) whose "lot is to be the pioneer women of this medium. Hardily," Spence says, "like our female frontier predecessors, we should stand strong and firm, remembering that we are actually paving the way for the grrls who will follow us" (Spence in Sinclair, 1996, p. xii). These women were among the first on the scene of "the new Wild Wild West ... still populated mostly by men and [running] basically on mob law" (p. x). This frontier metaphor has been discussed by a number of authors, among them Sutton (1996), who noted that "the net has been, and continues to be ... a masculine place, its atmosphere and protocol often being compared to the early days of the American West and the concept of 'frontier justice'" (p. 180).

Pioneers in an unknown and hostile space must be fearless and aggressive, defining and claiming their own territory. In her book, *Net Chick* (Sinclair, 1996), self-described by its author as "the only guide to stylish, post feminist, modern girl culture" (Ladd, 1996, par. 20), Sinclair was very clear about the qualities needed in this new frontier environment. Those who have inhabited it are:

> The progressive chicks who ... whipped out their machetes and cleared the way so that the rest of the sisterhood could easily enter the digital world. She told her readers that they would find the pioneer grrrls zooming down every lane on the Net [here the metaphors are getting a bit mixed] blasting through chat rooms and

newsgroups ... and creating incredibly hot pads ... where people
can drop by (if they dare!) to play with us. (Sinclair, 1996, p. 6)

Sinclair defined grrrls as women who don't "act like victims ...
[who] take responsibility for themselves ... enjoy their feminin-
ity and kick ass at the same time" (DeLoach, 1996).

Rosie X, an Australian described by Sinclair as "wickedly
sharp, mischievous, animated" described the Web as "a cool
place to be, an important place for grrrls to grab onto, get a foot-
hold, and help others to come on up." She noted that Aussies
were "tuff just like you American chicks" and that the two
countries "capture the psyche of adventurers" (Sinclair, 1996, p.
89). Asked why she chose *Geekgirl* as her site's name, Rosie responded that "if you're going to be damned for something any-
way, why not embrace it? Be proud of having tech skills instead
of embarrassed by it" (DeLoach, 1996).

This discourse is elitist and hierarchically motivated in its tendency to view the in group as explorers, first arrivals, and in the
vanguard. Cybergrrls have stepped forward to acquire technical
skills in a hostile environment and are now prepared to help their
less resourceful sisters. The frontier narrative thus excludes and
marginalizes newcomers who are not "in the know." Those who
can set aside their fears and act boldly (although belatedly) will
nonetheless benefit. Sherman (1997c) reinforced the metaphor of
taking control by concluding in one of her weekly columns that
"Computers and the Internet are tools for your life to connect you
to information and connect you to people. Taking control of computers and the Net means gaining access to these powerful tools
for research and communications" (par. 7). Taken together,
Sherman's site and others like it projected a masculinized gender
construction on their female readers.

The discourse of these women is an intriguing site of identity
construction and maintenance for Gen-Xers and colleagues
who have technical interests and skills. As DeLoach (1996) said
of them, they "exude attitude." Their chosen label, grrls, represents their desire to fight back against language such as *girl*,
bitch, and *honey* to make it clear, as one member of the group

said, that "we're not naked and we're not waiting for a hot chat" (DeLoach, 1996). Rosie X noted that she's always liked the grrowl in grrl and terms the language reclamation project a form of subtle subversion (DeLoach, 1996).

Cybergrrl narratives implicitly make use of dissociation to distinguish the technophile group of female Web site authors from the very group they are ostensibly trying to invite online. Cybergrrls are portrayed in their own self-descriptions and appeals as opportunistic, savvy, dynamic, resourceful, and forward looking. Absent and tacitly devalued are those women who are not technology literate or who are viewed as passive, unskilled, hesitant, or controlled by forces of which they themselves do not take control. The devalued terms of the value pairs implied in cybergrrl talk can be uncovered through attribution, but they also are disclosed by the cybergrrls in what they say. Rosie X noted that these Web site developers are "all too busy to have on line Tupperware parties" (DeLoach, 1996). Wertheim (1996) upbraided women for being "halted in [their] own passivity" and "apathetic" (p. 153) about computers and technology.

The frontier metaphor provided a framework for one commentator, L. Miller (1995), to discuss her concerns about new women coming online. She noted that the frontier "exists beyond the edge of settled or owned land," is viewed as "a lawless society of men, a milieu in which physical strength, courage, and personal charisma supplant institutional authority." She extended this idea by noting that "when civilization arrives on the frontier, it comes dressed in skirts" and that when women and children arrive "the law must follow because women and children must be protected" (pp. 51–52). It is here that Miller's agenda becomes apparent. She resents the print media's exploitation of the frontier metaphor to argue that the presence of vulnerable newcomers to the electronic milieu may require safeguards and protections for them, (i.e., regulation). Women, she argued, should be able to protect themselves, and the view that they are incapable of doing so reinforces gender stereotypes and puts the free-wheeling environment of the Internet at risk. Like Wertheim and the cybergrrls of *Net Chick*, Miller believes that women really ought to have more spunk than to believe that they need special protection.

Furthermore, the idea that women would retreat into women-only conferences and newsgroups disturbed L. Miller (1995): "In these laments I hear the reluctance of women to enter into the kind of robust debate that characterizes healthy public life.... Surely women can come up with a more spirited response than this" (p. 55). It is in her concluding paragraph that Miller's real agenda materializes:

> Women have always participated in on-line communications, women whose chosen careers in technology and the sciences have already marked them as gender-role resisters. As the schoolmarms arrive on the electronic frontier, their female predecessors find themselves cast in the role of saloon girls, their willingness to engage in "masculine" activities like verbal aggression, debate, or sexual experimentation marking them as insufficiently feminine or "bad" women. (p. 57)

Miller's views reveal an identifiable constituency of online women—those who pride themselves on independence, value free speech, know how to handle intimidation, feel comfortable with technology, and see CMC as an opportunity. They welcome their sisters to the new communication environment, but only so long as they are able to fend for themselves and become acculturated to the conventions, mores, and self-protections necessary to successful survival in the online environment. As long-time habitués of the Internet, Miller and the cybergrrls have already bought into its new libertarian ideology.

THE WEB'S CHANGING NATURE: E-ZINES AND OTHER ALTERNATIVES

During late 1996 and 1997, the Web opened up to women. Numerous noncommercial sites were developed that were designed for young women and teens. Some of these sites took the form of "zines," or in their electronic form, "e-zines." Such small magazines focused on aspects of female experience often ignored in the mainstream press. Richardson (1996) described them as a "forum for interacting with, reacting to, hacking up, and re-assembling pop culture." Popular e-zines included *Minx* (http://www.minxmag.com), *Bust* (http://www.bust.com), and *Maxi* (http://www.maximag.com).

Whereas the discourse and the posturing of cybergrrls appeared to be an effort to masculinize the feminine (i.e., to adopt identities colored by stereotypically male traits such as independence, aggression, and technological know-how), the discourse of these new sites rarely focused on technology per se. Instead, new site authors emphasized artistic expression (in writing and graphics), social support relevant to concerns of site visitors, music and film reviews, and gripes about coverage of women's issues in the popular press. In their efforts to appeal to Gen-Xers and to build a community based on shared interests, these e-zines also differed from politicized Web sites such as those posted by NOW (http://now.org/now/home.html) and the feminist Majority Foundation (http://www.feminist.org).

E-zines are indicative of a larger trend in Web publishing—the proliferation of sites designed for all sorts of constituencies. With the suppression of gatekeeping and the seemingly limitless capacity of the Web, people of various ethnicities, sexual orientations, political leanings, and interests are drawn to specific Web sites that have been posted with them in mind. Pursuing this chapter's focus on Web developments related to women's interests, I now briefly describe a few of the top-ranked women's sites developed in 1997 and 1998.[5]

Some highly ranked women's sites were commercial in the sense that they sought to market site authors' books, Web design services, and products. They also offered technical advice, professional networking opportunities, chat rooms, and forums for women. Prominent in this group is the aforementioned Cybergrrl Webstation where Aliza Sherman held forth in her weekly column and posted her comic strip (in which she was the

---

[5]Lycos ranks sites by content (quality of information), design (layout, presentation, quality of graphics) and overall (charm, entertainment value). WWWomen also gave awards to sites that were best in "content, inspiration, exploration, and presentation" ("Welcome," 1997).

heroine). Another popular commercial site was Amazon City
(http://www.amazoncity.com), which described itself as "femi-
nist/post feminist ... with a great sense of humor, a lack of political correctness ... smart, irreverent, but open-minded enough to
include content that might appeal to a large cross-section of
women (not just hip young urbanites)" ("Opportunities," 1998).
Amazon City was posted by Digital Amazon, a Web development studio that served corporate clients and nonprofit organizations and used its Web site to publicize its services.

Although noncommercial sites occasionally post product advertisements, their primary aim seems to have been to provide
resources for their readers and personal gratification for their authors and designers. Some of the top-ranked e-zines were very
professional in design, writing, and quality, and they also provided valuable information resources and forums for issues of interest to girls and young women. gURL (www.gURL.com), a
site designed for young teen girls, offered such features as an audio parody on sensitive guys by two sensitive guys, cartoons of
real-life teen gaffes and heartbreaks, tongue-in-cheek commentary on teen angst about sexuality, and an advice column that an-
swered the questions teen girls have always had but were
embarrassed to ask. Although sites such as these focused largely
on female concerns, they also attracted male readers because
they included writing by male authors and remained open to the
views and problems of young men.

Minx (www.minxmag.com) was a postfeminist e-zine for
Gen-Xers. One of its creators said that "we wanted to create a site
where you could look at clothes, read about sex, and not feel like
cheeseball sellout." The site was sexually explicit, with cruising
tips, birth control advice, boudoir reviews, and comics, but it was
nicely designed, clever, and easy to read. If one clicked there on
"relationships," one would be transported to "BreakupGirl"
(www.breakupgirl.com) a top-rated site that offered sanguine
advice about how to handle rejection. BreakupGirl ("When it's
over ... she'll be right over!") is available to come to the rescue.
The site was linked to the National Domestic Violence Hotline
for women in dangerous relationships, but for those in less dras-

tic straits, the site author offered advice on when to get out of relationships and how to get over being jilted or being the one doing the jilting. Nicely designed with gentle humor, the site surely would cheer its browsers and relieve depression in some.

These recently developed sites may be one reason more women sought out sites on the Web. They offered a forum for self-expression of all kinds, acknowledged and recognized creativity and originality, and (so long as one had the resources and desire to participate) did not exclude or marginalize their users. In their efforts to offer environments in which posters could feel safe, site authors proscribed inflammatory personal attacks ("flames"), harassing behavior, insults, and spamming. Insisting that participants in chat rooms and postings show respect for other communicators, such sites provided a comfortable environment for women. Furthermore, they provided an environment suited to the people who sought them out. Postfeminist sites were designed for those who want to "be smart AND to get laid" ("Minx Manifesto," 1998). gURL was suited to young teens insecure about their appearance, their social skills, and their sexuality. Other sites appealed to disgruntled housewives, lesbians, parents, ethnic minorities, and other groups. The sites have become sufficiently attractive, humorous, dynamic, and informative to attract a wide range of women (and men) from various demographic and income groups. Online, participants will find professional opportunities, information resources, new personal relationships, advice, and support. Commercial appeals, diatribes, sales pitches, and explicit persuasion did not bring many of the new participants online. Instead, new sites and developments on the Web itself invited them in.

CONCLUSION

The protechnology discourse and Web site activity described in this chapter have revealed two dimensions of communication on and about women's participation on the Internet. On one hand, media writers and online advocates exhorted women to get involved and to make use of new technologies. On the other hand, the content of new media changed and evolved into environments that were more open to women's ways of being in the world.

Rhetorical analysis of invitational rhetoric addressed to women to get them to come online showed that such talk and writing masculinized the feminine. That is, it constructed an "ideal" type of woman—one who was career oriented, opportunistic, and prepared to take risks and try new things. This discourse spoke of taking control of powerful tools and praised individuals who could take care of themselves on the new cyberspace frontier. By praising tech-savvy values and lifestyles and by upbraiding women who had other priorities (and thus were not interested), this invitational discourse ironically excluded some of the very audiences for which it was intended.

At the same time that these articles and web sites were first appearing, the Web was developing, and opportunities for new forms of involvement by women were growing. As Light (1995) observed, feminists may have been mistaken in portraying women only as victims of technology. Viewing the digital landscape as a "new space for women," Light noted the ways in which a technology can be redefined by redefining its potential uses. It would seem that many women (and men) are doing just that. They are using the Web to develop new modes of interacting with each other—providing a meeting space for parents who would otherwise be isolated in their homes, a space where employees can chat on their lunch hour, and a venue in which people of all kinds can publish their poetry and display their art. By engendering new uses for CMC, these new sites are "degendering the computer" (p. 134) and also constructing welcoming places where invitational discourse becomes truly inviting.

CHAPTER 3

Parody With a Purpose: Online Political Parody in the 2000 Presidential Campaign

Before the 2000 Presidential campaign got underway, George W. Bush's political advisors registered dozens of Internet domain names to preempt their use by Web site creators interested in political parody and satire. Bush's advisors thought of off-color and pejorative names, such as bushsucks.com and bushbites.com, but they neglected the innocuous gwbush.com, which was purchased by Zack Exley, a 29-year-old computer programmer from New York. By April 1999, Exley had established a Web site and begun lampooning Bush's supposed past drug use and political hypocrisy. The events that followed show that political parody can be a serious matter, as tactical errors by the Bush camp contributed to the popularity of Exley's site and gave it a national reputation.

The mistake that Bush and his advisors made was to call attention to the site. Shortly after it was posted, Benjamin L. Ginsberg, a lawyer for Bush's Exploratory Committee, sent a cease and desist order to Exley, claiming that gwbush.com violated copyright and trademark infringement laws. Then, in May 1999, Bush himself, in a televised news conference, called Exley a "garbage man" and said "there ought to be limits to freedom." (An audio clip of this statement was later posted on gwbush.com for users to hear for themselves.) Bush's statement raised the ire of many pro-free speech habitués of the Internet. To add to the fracas, Ginsberg later filed a complaint with the Federal Election Commission (FEC), claiming that Exley had used his site to advocate Bush's defeat.

Bush's efforts to shut down the site received a good deal of media attention from outlets such as the *Washington Post, The New York Times,* and the *Los Angeles Times.* Exley defended himself in news interviews, statements on his site, and a letter to the FEC (Exley, 1999; Neal, 1999). In the meantime, traffic on Exley's site increased from a trickle to over a million visitors in 1999. In April 2000, the FEC quietly dismissed Ginsberg's complaint, saying that it had more serious complaints to consider (Ritsch, 2000). The Bush campaign's actions in the matter had only served to draw attention to gwbush.com and make it one of the most, if not the most, sought-after parody sites in the 2000 presidential campaign. As Neal (1999) observed, "The Exley case demonstrates how, under the right circumstances, a lone dissenting voice can ruffle even the biggest feathers and how the Internet is playing a new role in the political process."

Although some observers might think that the Bush campaign's concern about gwbush.com was misplaced, subsequent events have shown that parodic activity can be a consequential factor in national campaigns. A number of well-designed parody sites appeared during the 2000 presidential primaries and remained active during the summer conventions and subsequent campaigns. Gwbush.com evolved into an elaborate site that included a new home page every few weeks and links to other Bush and Gore parody sites. This made it a sort of portal to parodic activity in the presidential campaign. Georgybush.com posted some exceedingly clever song parodies about Bush as a spoiled rich kid seemingly unconcerned about poor people and minorities. Algore-2000.org aired rather damning video clips about Gore's supposed incompetence and contradictory behavior. These sites used bona fide media reports to corroborate their content and provide a basis for ridicule. Visitors to the sites could learn a good deal about candidate biographies (most of it true) and have fun at the same time.

This chapter closely examines eight of the parody sites in the Bush–Gore race.[1] It emphasizes sites specifically concentrating on parody, defined as discursive activity that intentionally copies the style, organization, or other features of a text or situation, making its features more noticeable by way of humorous imitation (Cambridge Dictionaries Online, 2000). Even though these were not serious sites, they did appeal both to casual visitors and to a group of like-minded exchangers interested in the views of those who shared their values (B. Fisher, Margolis, & Resnick, 1996).[2]

These sites were entertaining and persuasive and, in my view, more interesting to visit than many of the serious sites. Even though by themselves they probably did not substantially influence the outcome of the election, they appeared to be quite popular. For example, gwbush.com reported 300,000 hits per month by mid-2000, and bushlite.net registered 48,610 visits during the same period and was averaging about 2,000 hits per week.[3] By revealing and documenting candidate contradictions on the issues, the sites provided a good deal of is-

---

[1]To select these sites, a research assistant and I browsed 12 to 15 anti-Bush sites. We then decided to focus on web sites emphasizing parody (as opposed to satire, scandal, or some other feature). Based on our preliminary browsing, we selected the terms "Bush," "parody," "dubya," and "campaign." We then ran six searches using two, three, or all four of these terms. The searches were run on Altavista, Google, Alltheweb, and Excite. These search engines placed consistently among the top five search engines since 1996, as reported by Notess (2000), a reviewer of search engine dynamics, methodologies, and rankings. Notess's rankings were based on database size, links and database reach, and total number of hits. Our search results were internally consistent and produced 11 sites that placed in the top 10 lists on one or more search engines. From this list, we eliminated sites that had not been updated in 2000, did not focus on parody, were pro-Bush, or no longer existed. This procedure produced a list of five sites: gwbush.com, bushlite.net, georgybush.com, bushcampaignhq.com, and youcrazy.com/georgewbush. We then followed the same procedure for Gore sites, searching for the terms "Gore," "parody," "bore," "snore," and "campaign." There were fewer Gore sites, and we selected three by applying the same criteria we had used on the Bush sites. These sites were allgore.com, algore-2000.org, and bradley-gore2000com. Our parody sites were selected in June and July 2000.

[2]B. Fisher et al. (1996) divided civic life on the Internet into five types: communitarian, democratic mobilization, like-minded exchange, technological elitism, and manipulation and domination. Parody sites would seem to fall in the third category where users "meet largely to discuss and promote their own interests and to reinforce their own like-mindedness ... with those who share their values" (p. 14).

[3]These totals are based on figures reported in Ritsch (2000) and on a counter displayed on the bushlite.net site.

sue-related information. By raising some well-founded questions about the candidates' past (e.g., Bush's alleged past drug use, Bush's and Gore's military activities during the Vietnam War, Gore's fundraising activities, etc.), the sites disclosed important biographical information. Because voters say that they are highly interested in the candidates' views on the issues and in their biographies, the sites' content was probably on target (George Washington University, 2000b).

After briefly discussing some aspects of the Internet's role in U.S. politics, this chapter describes and analyzes these parody sites and compares them with similar sites in the 1996 presidential campaign. The chapter has two purposes. The first is to show how these sites comprised a sort of discursive enclave held together by common sources, intertextual allusions, networked links, and intersite redundancies. The second purpose is to follow up on an earlier study of online parodic activity (Warnick, 1998a) by describing how forms of Web-based communication in this area have changed as the dynamics of the medium itself have changed.

The contributions of this chapter to critical literacy are in two forms. First, rhetorical criticism of Web site texts shows how coincidence and synchrony of texts can function to hail audiences of readers who are able to appreciate humor because of their ability to understand certain intertextual references and allusions. Second, comparison of 1996 and 2000 sites in the same category reveals in part how the nature of Web-based rhetorical activity has changed over time. Specifically, this comparison explains why discursive activity has become more constrained and more highly structured because of increased regulation and commercialization of the Internet.

POLITICAL PARTICIPATION
AND THE WORLD WIDE WEB

The advent of user activity on bulletin boards, listservs, and the Web in the early 1990s brought with it hope for increased involvement by citizens in politics. This hope was perhaps best described by Rheingold (1993) in his book *The Virtual Community*. In speaking of networks of communication, he noted:

> The political significance of CMC [computer-mediated communication] lies in its capacity to challenge the existing political hierarchy's monopoly on powerful communications media, and perhaps thus revitalize citizen-based democracy.... The distributed nature of the telecommunications network, coupled with the availability of affordable computers, makes it possible to piggyback alternate networks on the mainstream infrastructure. (p. 14)

Observers who were optimistic about expanding opportunities for political participation on the Internet emphasized its lack of structure, convenience, interactive capacity, and ease of access for those who wanted to get their message out.

For the past 5 to 6 years, the research of some political scientists has examined whether the Internet has indeed made greater citizen involvement possible. The researchers' conclusions thus far were well expressed by Davis (1999) when he noted that "rather than acting as a revolutionary tool rearranging political power and instigating direct democracy, the Internet is destined to become dominated by the same actors in American politics who currently utilize other mediums" (p. 5). The consensus is that certain well-resourced and established interests who dominated media and public discourse prior to the Internet have simply migrated online. These interests include major media conglomerates, political parties, commercial businesses, government agencies, and interest groups. There are at least three reasons why the Internet has come to be viewed as a less open and accessible communication environment than people had originally hoped it might be.

First, in terms of citizen access, the World Wide Web has come to the forefront of Internet activity, and as of early 2001, it has become largely a broadcast medium emphasizing information and strategic messages rather than interpersonal communication. Resnick (1997) argued that "despite all the hype about interactivity, Web Browsers and Home Pages were also responsible for transforming the Net into a relatively passive medium, significantly more passive than the one envisioned by those who celebrate the Web as a spectacular breakthrough in interactivity" (p. 51). Political sites on the Web are usually viewed as venues for posting information rather than forums for exchanging views with constituents or enabling groups of people to communicate with each other. In a 1998 study of 161 campaign Web sites, the Democracy Online Project found that only 81 sites had e-mail on the home page and only 28 responded to e-mail within 24 hours (George Washington University, 2000a). Another 1998 research survey on online political activity reported that only 15% of respondents had expressed a political or social opinion through an e-mail list or bulletin board, and only 11% had participated in an online discussion about politics (Pew Research Center for People and the Press, 1998). The Web sites discussed in this chapter attempted to simulate interactivity through invitations to e-mail the Webmaster, unmonitored message boards, invitations to contribute to the site, and sales of goods and services. Although such features may stimulate user interest and involvement, they are not the same as online interactive discussion or chat.

Second, the possibilities for freer access to the public forum by individuals and small groups have not lived up to expectations. It has been said that anyone (with the requisite resources and skills) can post a Web site, and that is true. Because of the increasing structuration and organization of the Internet, however, merely posting a Web site is an entirely different matter from posting a successful and frequently visited site. Zack Exley's experience with gwbush.com is an excellent example of the problem. In his letter to the FEC regarding the complaint against him in June 1999, Exley reported that he had recently had to increase the fees he paid to his hosting service (because of increased site traffic), retain legal counsel, and invest considerably more time in maintaining the site (Exley, 1999). In addition, individuals and interests seeking access to an audience of any size usually have to have sites that are professionally designed and then need to get their sites reviewed and ranked by major search engines. All of this entails major investments of time, energy, and money.

Third, many political scientists claim that most Americans follow politics only peripherally and are largely politically apathetic. To the extent that they do attend to politics, their focus tends to be narrow and centered on only a few issues. Bimber (1998) observed that "the Net will not alter the fact that most people are highly selective in their attention to political issues and their assimilation of political information." Others have observed that most voters pay attention to elections only in the waning days of the campaign and that "for most voters, information comes from snippets of newspaper stories or campaign brochures hung on the doorknob" (Davis, 1999, p. 179). People who are busy with work, family, and leisure activities often do not make time for politics and are unlikely to spend their time online seeking out political information.

It could be, however, that prospects for a major change in politics because of the Internet are not as dim as research has thus far indicated. As I noted in chapter 1, in the mid-1990s when Bimber's and Davis's research was done, the Internet population was limited in size and dominated by affluent, well-educated, and technically astute adult male users. In 1996, only 23% of Americans were connected to the Internet; in late 1999, more than 55% were connected (Harris Interactive, 1999; Nie & Erbring, 2000; Pew Research Center for People and the Press, 1998). Furthermore, studies of Internet use patterns indicate that people spend more hours on the Internet the more years they have been online (Nie & Erbring, 2000). The more time people spend online, the wider their range of Internet-based activities becomes. A common user pattern is to begin by using e-mail and then to start using the Internet and specifically the Web to locate information, support hobbies, and seek entertainment. Younger users—children and adolescents—are the most frequent users of games and chat and seem to prefer online synchronous interaction more than adults (Nie & Erbring, 2000).

As personal computers become cheaper, Internet access becomes more widespread, and younger users become adults, patterns of use may change and the Internet may have a greater impact on political activity. In the late 1990s, some observers believed that availability of access to the Internet was

already beginning to have an effect. In 1998, when Jesse
Ventura ran for governor of Minnesota, he used limited financial resources, one paid staffer, and an amateur Web techni-
cian to mobilize 3,000 volunteers for rallies that generated
media coverage that advanced his candidacy (Neal, 1999).
During the 2000 presidential primaries, John McCain's Web
site drew in more than $2.2 million in contributions in 1 week,
and e-mail contacts through the site were vital in recruiting
campaign volunteers (Shogren, 2000).

The technical capacities of the Net to support online registration and voting have also improved. After a number of straw
polls, the first incident of online voting occurred in Arizona in
March 2000 when Democrats in a presidential preference primary voted online. Nearly 40,000 members of the electorate
voted this way, and reported turnout and minority group representation substantially increased (Election.com, 2000; White,
2000). Sixty percent of respondents to a recent poll said they
would be more likely to vote if they could vote online, and the
White House has asked the National Science Foundation to
study the possibility of online voting ("What on Earth?," 2000).
If problems related to security, minority access, and socioeco-
nomic status can be solved, Internet voting may become commonplace, increasing convenience of and access to political
participation.

In any case, surveys of Internet activity in the 2000 presidential campaign showed that many attentive voters depended on
political sites for information. A Gallup poll of 596 Internet users in February 2000 revealed that 23% had used the Internet to
look up information about the presidential campaign, 30% had
used it to follow news about the campaign, and 16% felt that
Internet resources had helped them be a better voter (Gallup
Organization, 2000). In light of these data and the counts of
Web site visits to gwbush.com and other parody sites, it is quite
likely that online presidential parodies drew the attention of interested voters throughout the campaign period.

The eight parody sites included in this chapter were designed
to attract users' attention and keep them on the sites and inter-

ested in what they had to say. Although some site designs were copied from the original official sites (and therefore were not themselves original), they were attractive and easy to use. The sites were also convenient venues to learn about candidate gaffes and foibles because they provided candidate biographies and chronological accounts of some aspects of campaign histories. Two sites—gwbush.com and algore-2000.org—also had depth, featuring video clips, audio clips, and links to press coverage of candidate statements and activities. Most sites provided links to other sites featuring scandals, satire, and parody. As the rest of this chapter shows, the parody sites were not only a "a nice place to visit," but a self-reinforcing environment where like-minded individuals could share what they knew and enjoy a chuckle at the same time.

BUSH–GORE PARODY SITES: "SAYING" SOMETHING WHILE SAYING NOTHING

Parodists' work in the 2000 presidential election campaign was made more difficult by the actions taken by Bush forces against the gwbush.com Web site. The cease and desist order, the FEC complaint, as well as possibilities of lawsuits for copyright infringement against site authors seemed to have a chilling effect on parodic activity. In midsummer 2000, just prior to the Republican and Democratic national conventions, some sites seemed to have been abandoned or neglected. Update information indicated that, after the Super Tuesday runoffs, some Webmasters stopped actively maintaining their sites. Bushcampaignhq.com and bushlitc.net were in a quiescent state with the occasional exception of postings to message boards. On the other side, anti-Gore activity was no higher, with three sites (youcrazy.com/algore2000, albore.com, and bore2000.com) becoming dysfunctional or nonexistent.

Those sites that were active specialized in producing discourse without overtly making claims of any sort. That is, they avoided propositional statements (e.g., "Al Gore is a political advantage seeker" or "George Bush is uncaring and immature")

and instead conveyed their content through implication.[4] There
are a number of strategies for implicit communication, of which
parody is one. Site authors also created fictional candidates ("G.
W. Bush" and "Bushlite"), exposed contradictions between candidates' words and actions, invited visitors to contribute material
to their sites, fabricated fictional narratives and "news releases,"
and linked to other sites specializing in caricature or visual parody. In addition, Bush site authors constantly included disclaimers such as "this article is completely fictional," or "this site is a
parody," not only to protect themselves, but to remind readers of
the spirit of seriousness in which the Bush camp had tried to quell
or discourage parodic activity. Because avoidance of explicit as-
sertion is a prominent characteristic of parody, Web sites critical
of Gore used the same technique, but not as religiously as the
Bush sites did. The remainder of this section describes the various ways in which site authors used parody, caricature, external
commentary, and multimedia to expose the candidates' flaws
and foibles.

The thrust of parodic activity for both candidates was to con-
vey a sense of each man's character—or rather, the lack thereof.
Some polls of voters prior to the runoff election showed that
people considered the personal qualities of a candidate as important in their voting decision, with honesty, caring about
them, and leadership as significant qualities (Lester, 2000). For
voters attending to personal character, the 2000 parody sites
were a rich source of information. Bush (nicknamed "Shrub")
was generally portrayed as immature, a daddy's boy, clueless,
unintelligent, inexperienced, hypocritical, and a rich kid. Gore
(also referred to as "Tree") was viewed as a bragger, a liar, stiff,
hypocritical, and without substance.

One means of viewing the candidates' character was
through their speech. In the spirit of parody, site authors fabricated speech that copied the candidates' styles and patterns of
speaking in ways that revealed their weaknesses. For example,

---

[4]An additional motivation for avoiding claims about the candidates was that sites that
did not advocate the defeat or election of candidates could avoid FEC regulations. (I am in-
debted to Jason Edward Black for this observation.)

the work of Bush parodists was made easier by the comparatively vacuous welcoming statement prominently displayed on
Bush's real home page:

> Welcome to georgewbush.com—my virtual campaign headquar-
> ters. The most important question I can answer for you is why I am
> running for President of the United States. I am running for Presi-
> dent because our country must be prosperous. But prosperity must
> have a purpose. The purpose of prosperity is to make sure the Amer-
> ican dream touches every willing heart. The purpose of prosperity is
> to leave no one out—to leave no one behind. I'm running because
> my political party must match a conservative mind with a compas-
> sionate heart. And I'm running to win. (Bush for President, 2000)

The bushlite.net site earmarked these paragraphs (which continued to lead off the official Bush site even after it was redesigned in Summer 2000) for special ridicule. Noting that "Bush"
had appointed rapper Vanilla Ice as Director of Alliteration for
his campaign, the parodic site included some of Ice's suggested
phrases: "Frat Boy for Freedom," "Execution for Excellence,"
and "Governing for the Greedy." These phrases drew attention
to the facile style of Bush's welcome but also to his privileged
childhood, role as governor of the state with the highest execution rate, representative of Big Oil, and big fund raiser.
Bushlite.net further capitalized on Bush's text in a fabricated announcement speech said to have been given in June 1999:

> Prosperity is not a given. That wouldn't be prosperous, nor would
> it have a purpose. What's the purpose of giving out prosperity to
> just anyone? Purposeful prosperity—that is prosperity with a pur-
> pose—must be earned. To earn it, we need compassionate conser-
> vatism. By this I mean conservatism that is also compassionate.
> (DieTryin.com, 2000)

This reduction to the absurd foregrounds the euphemistic quality and circularity of Bush's original statement, and it also de-
codes it by indicating that "purposeful" prosperity really is not
for everyone but only for those positioned to benefit from
trickle-down resources. It also capitalizes on Bush's presum-

ably unfortunate choice of "compassionate" to accompany "conservative." For some audiences, the emphasis on compassion would imply that caring and supportiveness are rare in conservative candidates.

This level of ridicule intensified on the youcrazy.com/ georgewbush site, which appropriated the logos, frames, coloring, and photos from the official Bush site but substituted new text projecting "Bush Junior" as selfish, petulant, and apathetic. The site's lead story reported that Bush was threatening to stop his campaign and spend $54 million in campaign contributions to outfit a professional NASCAR racing car team. Its parody of the welcome announcement had Bush admitting that "I was fine with the whole compassionate conservative bit.... But ya know what? This country doesn't NEED a compassionate conservative. What it needs is a kick in the ass" (You Crazy!, 2000). The "En Español" link on this site produced a message prompt that said: "Yo, Jose, welcome to America. Now learn the damned language." In the "On the Road" link, Bush complained about kissing babies ("Keep the nasty things away from me"), shaking hands, and listening to the "Star Spangled Banner" ("If I could go back in time, Francis would be a DEAD man"). Through pseudo-speech, the site alluded to Bush's all-White, prep school upbringing, his playboy image, and his infatuation with sports. The plethora of diminutives attributed to him in other parody pages ("bushlite," "georgybush," "littlegeorgebush"), along with allusions to Bush Senior ("Following Poppy's Footsteps," "Heir to the Throne") never let readers forget his status as Bush Junior.

Unfortunately for the opposing camp, Al Gore also offered an easy target for parody, partially because his speeches have a nearly inevitable pattern of characteristics with little variety. His usual organization is to identify a problem, use a personal story to dramatize it, explain what the Clinton administration accomplished, cite facts and figures to show progress, and then conclude by describing his own new initiatives. This pattern is evident in excerpts from one of Gore's bona fide speeches on crime.

All too often, I have seen how crime and violence can tear families and communities apart. I have comforted parents who have lost their children to gun violence. I have heard the powerful testimony of women who have been victims of domestic violence....

I pledge to you today: if I am entrusted with the Presidency, I will launch a sweeping anti-crime strategy to make our families safe and secure. I will intensify the battle against crime, drugs, and disorder in our communities. I've been in this fight for a long time now.... President Clinton and I believed that we needed a tougher, more comprehensive strategy, to fight crime on every single front....

We're putting 100,000 new community police officers on the street, all across this country. We funded new prison cells, and expanded the death penalty for cop killers and terrorists.... Now we see the results of that strategy: serious crime is down seven years in a row, to its lowest level in a quarter-century. (Gore 2000, 2000)

Gore concluded this speech by promising a national crime policy, including more police, tougher laws, judicial reform, increased drug treatment, and victims' rights protections. This formulaic and repetitive pattern is also predictable and tedious. When combined with Gore's stiff delivery, it is probably a contributing factor to Gore's reputation as an uninteresting speaker. Furthermore, parodists could also easily plug in content of all kinds and produce very Gorian-sounding results. For example, here is a play on Gore's proenvironment stance:

I am painfully aware of the plight of the small forest creatures. Unlike deer and eagle, creatures like snails and worms simply cannot move fast enough to outrun a Forestry Service set fire. That is why I led the charge to create the "Small Creatures of the Forest" recovery fund.

This fund organizes and pays for the repatriation of millions of small and microscopic creature eggs into millions of public and private acres that the forestry department burns every year. (bradley-gore2000.com, 2000)

Another site (allgore.com) produced a speech announcing a partnership to redecorate 1 million homes. Noting that more than two thirds of families don't like their homes, "Gore" proposed a plan to spruce up lawns, clean sidewalks, put 100,000 pink flamingoes on the streets, modernize 5,000 bird baths, and build more parks and green spaces (All Gore, 2000).

Such parodies highlighted the Clinton–Gore predisposition to want to solve most problems with a government-funded program. They also reminded readers that Gore's thinking often seemed unimaginative and, well, boring. In addition, Gore's tendency to exaggerate his own past accomplishments in these speeches and elsewhere provided opportunities for parodists to point out the exaggerations, much to Gore's disadvantage. The most noticeable example of this was his claim (from a March 1999 interview with Wolf Blitzer) that "during my service in the United States Congress, I took the initiative in creating the Internet" (algore-2000.org, 2000). This claim was, and was viewed as, counterfactual, because funding for development of the Internet was known to have started in 1969 when its predecessor, ARPANET, first went online (Castells, 1996). A video clip of this statement from the Blitzer interview was available on the algore-2000.org Web site, and other claims Gore had made about his record in Congress were elsewhere exposed as false. These included his claim to have "discovered" Love Canal (which was declared a disaster area during the Carter administration before Gore got involved) and his claim to have authored the earned income tax credit legislation that became law a year before Gore entered Congress (algore-2000.org, 2000). A visitor to algore-2000.org who saw its videos and reported misstatements would have to conclude that Gore either had a seriously faulty memory or was inclined to stretch the truth, or both.

The Web offers some unique opportunities for parody that distinguish it from print and other media. For example, the content of official candidate home pages—including text, design, and graphic identity—is something of which many users are very aware. Therefore, parodies of home page speeches and photos can be effective because of users' familiarity with the original home page texts.[5] Furthermore, the process of Web page construction makes it easy for site designers to appropriate selective portions of official site home pages and then use them for their own parodic purposes. The skill of such appropriations is one more aspect of parody that can be appreciated by users and readers who are in the know about the larger political scene on the Web at any point in time.

Another fruitful resource for parodists of both Gore and Bush was the candidates' propensity for malapropism and misstatement. A news article linked from the bushcampaignhq.com site noted that, when it came to Bush malapropisms, "the syntax of the father has been visited on the son." Bush's penchant for malapropism emerged in references to Greeks as "Grecians," Kosovars as "Kosovarians," and Slovenians as "Slovakians." Bush warned his constituents that quotas would "vulcanize society," and he coined new English terms such as "tacular," "mential," and "bariffs" (I I. Kennedy & Siemaszko, 2000). Gore, on the other hand, noted of President Bush in 1992 that "a zebra does not change its spots." In an effort to thank a largely Hispanic audience in 1996, Gore walked on stage and said "Machismo gracias." In 1994, he noted that the effort to build a collective civic space could fulfill the idea "that we can be e pluribus unum—out of one, many" (algore-2000.org, 2000). Not only were such errors described and posted on the parody sites, they also provided ways to mimic and mock the candidates' speech.

In addition to purely verbal parody, effective use was made of multimedia on the parody sites. The more technically sophisticated sites deployed animated Graphic Interchange Format (GIFs), audio and video clips, and digitized photographs, often used to enmesh the candidates in webs of their own making. For example, the aforementioned audio clip of Bush saying "There ought to be limits to freedom" was posted on gwbush.com's home page (gwbush.com, 2000). The same site also posted fabricated audios such as "Death Watch," about an alarm that rings

---

[5]The home pages for both Bush and Gore were substantially redesigned in midsummer 2000 when the vice presidential running mates were announced. At that point, the parodists' mimicry of the candidates' original home pages became less apparent.

every time there's an execution in Texas and "A Wing and a Prayer" about Bush's service in Texas in the Air National Guard during the Vietnam War. By coupling these with GIFs and images of Bush guzzling beer, Bush with a bong, Bush standing in his National Guard uniform with his leg propped on a beer keg, and so on, the site conveyed the clear impression that Bush is a party animal. To the extent that this site was successful, it was so because it selected a few themes (draft dodging, alleged cocaine use, hypocrisy, education governor) and consistently stayed with them throughout the site.

Algore-2000.org made things even more difficult for the hapless Gore. Near the top of this site's home page were links for eight video clips that featured, for example, the claim about inventing the Internet from the Blitzer interview, Gore's inability to recall the White House URL, and an incident in which Gore could not recognize likenesses of the founding fathers at Monticello (algore-2000.org, 2000). Most damaging were two clips from a Gore speech at the 1996 Democratic convention about his sister's illness and death from cancer and her smoking. In the first clip, Gore pledged to combat youth smoking. This clip was counterposed to a clip of a campaign stump speech Gore made in Tennessee after his sister's death in which he claimed common ground with tobacco farmers:

> Throughout most of my life, I raised tobacco. I want you to know that with my own hands, all of my life, I put it in the plant beds and transferred it. I've hoed it, I've dug it, I've sprayed it, I've chopped it, I've shredded it, spiked it, put it in the barn and stripped and sold it. (algore-2000.org, 2000)

This use of audio clips, photography, and videos from other sources again illustrates the unique opportunities for parody offered by Internet-based technologies. These multimedia clips furnished the original texts that site authors could subsequently parodize. Media convergence (use and adoption of various forms of media in other media) has become commonplace (Bolter & Grusin, 1999), and the Bush–Gore parodists made a fine art of placing digital video and audio strategically on their sites. Use of the Bush audio about limits to free speech on the gwbush.com site drew special attention to Bush's derogation of a value near and dear to many Internet users. The juxtaposing of Gore's heart-rending story about his sister's death from lung cancer next to his stump speech to the tobacco farmers was particularly powerful rhetorically and made him look like an inveterate hypocrite.

Gore's habit of remaking his image and shifting his stand on issues when it seemed politically convenient made it appear that there was no "there" there—a condition also subject to parodic commentary:

> Since the conviction of his good friend, Maria Hsia, Gore has reached out to independent voters by remaking himself in the image of John McCain. When it became clear that most voters were not responding favorably to the change in strategy, the Gore campaign decide [sic] to alter their course again, this time remaking him in the image of Jesse Ventura. As part of this new effort Gore has shaved his head and begun working on changing his phony Southern drawl to a thick Minnesota accent. (BSNN.net, 1999)

To dramatize these self-imposed transformations, new Web building tools made it possible to intermix images—a Bradley–Gore composite or a Clinton–Gore composite. Superimposing images allowed Gore's face to appear on Mt. Rushmore, Bush's head to appear on a king's body ("heir" to the throne), and Bush-ified Beverly Hillbillies with Dubya as Jethro driving the car and the rest of the Bush clan personae superimposed on the characters. Audio clips of parodic songs were accompanied by displayed lyrics with external links embedded to support allusions made in the lyrics. Tipper Gore the censor was pictured as "Titters" with superimposed bare chest blacked out. There were also unmodified photos of Gore in Beijing and at the Buddhist temple campaign fund raiser.

The relatively few Gore sites still active just prior to the Democratic convention were a circumscribed discursive universe with a set of circulating commonplaces (e.g., inventor of the Internet, Tipper Gore as censor, policy flip-flops, illusory career accomplishments) documented and established through video clips, prior media coverage, and voting records. This set of commonplaces then provided the raw materials for spin-off parody (e.g., bare-breasted Titters Gore, "In Chinese" link, fabricated speeches, and outlandish and trivial policy ideas).

To a lesser extent, the same was true of the Bush parody sites, although there were more of them, and there was more variety as well. Bush's supposed privileged childhood, connections with Big Oil, support for capital punishment, past alcohol abuse, and his claims to be a "compassionate conservative" were all thematized by the parodists. Partly as a result of the cease and desist letter and the FEC complaint against gwbush.com, site authors evaded hostile actions against them by Bush forces by relying on other voices to make their points. They invited letters and contributions from site users; encouraged postings to their message boards; linked to media coverage of Bush gaffes; constructed fabricated songs, stories, and speeches; published pseudo-polls; sold parodizing stickers, buttons, and t-shirts; and consistently reminded readers very explicitly that what they were doing had no basis in fact. By not overtly "saying" anything for which they could be held accountable, they said a great deal.

TEXTUALITY: CONTROLLING THE READER'S POINT OF VIEW

Despite the dispersed, multimediated environment in which they worked, parodic site authors in the 2000 presidential race appeared to succeed in controlling their readers' points of view and getting their message across. In a hypertext environment, this is generally not easy. Web sites are often broken into lexias (small blocks of text), with embedded internal links to other sites that relate to or support the site of origin. The emphasis is on "offering discrete constituent bits of information; these bits do not become narrative until the reader arranges and joins them" (Travis, 1996). Coherence and unity of rhetorical intent can splay out until the reader stops paying attention and moves on to some other site of interest. This expansion is a danger, as

Coover (as cited in Travis, 1996) noted when he observed that hypertext "runs the risk of being so distended and slackly driven as to lose its centripetal force" (that which centers and unifies the thought). Site authors thus have at least two challenges: to sustain reader attention and simultaneously to give the reader the illusion that he or she is freely constructing the text. As I noted elsewhere (Warnick, 1998a), the experience of Web browsing is often like playing a game or solving a puzzle. So long as the reader is held in suspense and cannot predict the outcome, the reader remains interested. The trick is to construct virtual experiences that sustain reader activity. In one variant of this strategy, the reader begins by encountering the unfamiliar, then starts to understand through play and experiment, then reduces uncertainty as content becomes familiar, then figures out the calculus by which the game is played (Friedman, 1995). The reader who started as a stranger to the topic is transformed into one who is "in the know" through various experiential devices.

One of the ways in which parody works, of course, is to draw on an already-recognized style or textual format to parodize the original text, as shown in my earlier example of how parodists mocked Gore's speech. Beyond that, however, parodists' use of intertextuality and recognizable speech genres also contributed to a sense of play and constructed a reader "in the know." Home pages of some of the more sophisticated parody sites were quick to draw reader attention to candidate words and actions that later were used to make them look foolish. By making these "bytes" salient for readers, parodists could provide interpretive frames for what they said elsewhere, as well as bases for allusions and forms of speech readers could later recognize and enjoy.

Within this network of parody sites, various forms of intertextuality made oblique references to external texts appearing elsewhere on the sites or in the political arena. Intertextuality is a form of interreference among texts in which an already-familiar text is invoked or played on in a new textual context.[6] Intertextuality can act as an intersection of texts through various kinds of anterior or synchronic utterances (Bizzell & Herzberg, 1990). For example, the bumper sticker slogan "Read my lips, no new Bushes" (gwbush.com) is a play on the elder George Bush's pledge, "Read my lips, no new taxes" (on which he later renegged). The subtitle of the Bushlite.net site was "Parody with a purpose" (a play on "prosperity with a purpose"), and the subtitle of Bradley-gore2000.com was "Because a zebra can't change it's [sic] spots," a play on Gore's aforementioned criticism of the senior Bush in 1992. Although intertextuality has been discussed in terms of its potential for opening up texts in a synchronic play of signs in cultural context (Landow, 1997), in the case of these parodic sites, intertextual references worked as they did because they invoked textual connections recognizable to habitual readers of sites knowledgeable about campaign satire and parody. They functioned successfully by virtue of their placement in a bounded and circumscribed discursive universe.

Because many sites had no identifiable author, the intertextual cross-references appearing on a site or in links to sites provided some coherence to the experience of reading these parodic sites. The frames and link patterns on the algore-2000.org site were taken from those on the algore2000.com official site. The same was true of the youcrazy.com/georgewbush site, which freely took its design, frames, logo, coloring, and even photos from the official Bush site. Regular visitors to the Bush parody sites also knew that bushsucks.com, one of the URLs purchased earlier by the Bush campaign, would take them directly to Bush's official campaign site. These visitors would know that Bush handlers had purchased this Web address specifically to forestall the very sort of parody made possible by the surrogate URL.

---

[6]Ott and Walter (2000) noted that feminist critics such as Julia Kristeva and media scholars each use the term intertextuality to refer to two distinct phenomena. The first form of intertextuality refers to an interpretive practice unconsciously used by audiences—a sensibility that conceives of texts as fragments in a larger web of textuality. The second refers to stylistic devices consciously used to make specific lateral associations between texts. It is this second form of lateral reference that was strategically used by the political parodists discussed in this chapter.

Although some features of these sites, such as their design, circulating commonplaces ("prosperity with a purpose," "inventor of the Internet," "compassionate conservativism," etc.), and intertextual references gave them unity, they were nevertheless a highly heteroglossic environment. *Heteroglossia* is use of "another's speech in another's language" to express authorial intentions in a refracted way (Bakhtin, 1981, p. 324). Bakhtin was concerned with discursive forms in the novel where authors speak in their characters' voices; dialogues are reported; and the discourse of letters, diaries, sermons, confessions, and all manner of speech genres are produced. As Bakhtin (1981) described it, "the author utilizes now one language, now another in order to avoid giving himself up wholly to either of them" (p. 314).

Like some novels, the scene on parodic Web sites was truly cacophonous. They included various genres of speech, among them the disclaimer ("Remember this is not the real George Bush site. These letters are fictitious. We're putting them here for fun. Don't sue us."), fabricated speeches ("It's so nice to be back here in Chumpville [WILD APPLAUSE]. Thank you. Now let me tell you why I care so much about every one of you here in Chumpville."), and faux news stories ("Bush Lite Announces Formation of Exploratory Committee to Study the Possibility of Establishing Steering Committee to Explore Potential Preliminary Position Statements"). Such forms of speech, constructed by site authors, were accompanied by others' actual news stories, postings to site message boards, the Texas Republican Party platform, computer games, parody songs, banner ads, and ads for site-related merchandise such as campaign buttons, bumper stickers, and t-shirts (each with their own logos).

The use of various recognizable speech forms and genres (e.g., the bumper sticker, the party platform, the frequently asked question, the pseudo-poll, the news clip) provided opportunities for reader participation and interactivity. By exploiting the various strata of speech, parodic sites involved their readers as they responded to others' messages, voted in parody polls, watched videos, listened to songs, played computer games, and purchased merchandise. Although opportunities for synchronous interaction with other users or with the candidates were unavailable, most parodic sites nonetheless felt very lively. If "diversity of speech is the ground of style" (Bakhtin, 1981, p. 303), then many site authors exploited its potential for comic effect.

The sites nevertheless had an underlying agenda and rhetorical point of view. Site authors clearly sought to turn their readers against the lampooned candidates or, if not that, at least to raise questions in readers' minds about the candidates' character, integrity, and intentions. Despite some critical theorists' views that hypertext can open up the text to "an apparently infinite play of relationships" (T. E. Morgan, cited in Landow, 1997, p. 35) or use "multiplicity and expansiveness [to] enable readers to expand the text" (Travis, 1996) parodic site authors sought to control their readers' points of view. They did this not through direct appeal or explicit argument, but by strategically using embedded links, multimedia clips, intertextual allusions, careful site designs, and contrived interactive features.

THE CHANGING POLITICAL WEB: PARODY IN 1996 AND 2000

Web-based political parody in the 2000 presidential campaign was a small sector of political activity on the Internet at that time. Although it is not possible to generalize broadly from this limited sample, close study of one kind of political discourse offers the opportunity to examine how the ways in which Web texts operate have been changing. Although few observers would disagree that the Web has changed dramatically since the 1990s, comparing these 2000 sites with the ones posted 4 years before in the 1996 presidential campaign helps us to understand the nature of those changes more clearly. The purpose of this section of the chapter is to explain how parodic activity has become more strategic and more overtly rhetorical because of changes in the nature of the Web itself.

First, parodic political sites in 1996 were less structured and more haphazardly designed than those in 2000. Web sites parodying Bob Dole and Bill Clinton in 1996 were posted by hobbyists interested in expressing themselves on the Web for their own and others' entertainment (Warnick, 1998a). Their sites were small and relatively disorganized. They interspersed external links to other sites with internal links to their own. Thus, in the middle of browsing a site, one could find oneself somewhere else, on another parody site, or lost and disoriented. Although site posters probably wanted users to read their sites, they did not seem committed to controlling their readers' point of view.

By 2000, the conditions in which Web site parodists worked had changed. As the Web became more commercialized, the need for infrastructure and wherewithal to build, post, maintain, and update a site had increased. To offset the expenses of server storage, site management, copyright fees, and legal representation, designers of larger sites had to sell merchandise or advertising space on their sites. They therefore needed to keep users on their sites, and so internal links to their content and site design features that kept their users oriented were necessary. On the other hand, external links to other parodic sites increased the originating site's ranking by search engines and thus its visibility. Therefore, a site such as Zack Exley's gwbush.com became a portal to other parodic sites simply by posting links to any and every other parodic site on Bush and Gore on its home page. Linking patterns themselves are a form of rhetorical activity. Organized external links make a site into a portal, whereas well-planned internal links keep the user on the site once he or she has become interested in its content.

A second point of comparison between the 1996 and 2000 parodic sectors arose from the potential for litigation. In 1996, parodists freely engaged in slander, innuendo, and allegation against major party candidates. They circulated accusations of political plots and behind-the-scenes maneuvering without support or corroboration (Warnick, 1998a). Furthermore, parodic activity in 1996 began early in the campaign and escalated over time, both in the number of sites and the allegations made.

In 2000, things were very different. After the primaries, few new sites were posted. Perhaps because of the Bush campaign's FEC complaint and threatened lawsuit against Zack Exley, the remaining parodists were fairly meticulous about what they parodied and how. As I have noted, they used disclaimers, supporting links to nonparodic news coverage, or fictional political characters to avoid litigation. Also, a number of sites went dormant. Without periodic updates or added material, only their message boards (for which they would be less likely to be held responsible) remained active.

A major shift in rhetorical activity on these sites can therefore been seen in the contrast between the 1996 and 2000 sites. The emergence of the Web as a mass medium, reaching up to 60% of the general public, has meant that those people who want to engage in meaningful parody and do it successfully must be prepared to invest money, time, and labor. These requirements can cause the hobbyist to drop out of the picture or to see his or her site recede into obscurity because no one can find it. As Tetzlaff (2000) observed:

> Under the rules and definitions the Web has already adopted, the "best" sites—the ones that look the sharpest, perform the most tricks, have the most bandwidth—will belong to the people that have the most resources to spend on these things. It's not just that amateurs don't have the talent or money to operate at this level, it's that they don't have the time. (p. 10)

The colonization of the Internet by government regulation, corporate investment, and litigation since the mid-1990s has made it into a much less free-wheeling and open environment. Many studies have predicted and commented on this development (Bolter & Grusin, 1999; Jordan, 1999; S. E. Miller, 1996). This chapter has used textual analysis and comparison with conditions in 1996 to show how this has occurred.

Noting the continuities as well as the differences in parodic Web site activity in 1996 and 2000 is also informative. Although this chapter has examined only a small portion of political activity on the Web in these two campaigns, it is nonetheless a potentially significant portion. The 2000 Web sites in this sector alone had hundreds of thousands of hits during the primary and runoff election periods. They evidently attracted a following of users who enjoy political humor. These sites offered a mixed contribution to political discourse in the two campaigns. They may have attracted people (particularly young people) who would have been uninterested in nonparodic sites and issue-based analysis. The 2000 sites' extensive reliance on nonparodic news coverage of the candidates' beliefs and activities probably served to inform users, particularly younger users, about the presidential contest; that is, they may have drawn users' attention to the contest between Bush and Gore.

However, some of the same criticisms I made of the parodic sites in 1996 still applied. First, by emphasizing ridicule, misstatements, gaffes, hypocrisy, and misdeeds of the two candidates, the parodic sites played into the public's belief that politicians are corrupt, dishonest, and not to be respected. Second, as I noted in 1998, a good deal of the interactivity on parodic Web sites is ineffective. Users' participation in Web site polls, online chat, and message boards may raise their level of interest and keep them on the site, but it is unlikely to meaningfully influence the outcome of the campaigns. Users' time might be better spent in other forms of online and offline political activity, such as canvasing, volunteering, reading about the issues, and actually voting. My conclusion, then, is that online political parody might attract and interest some people who otherwise might be uninvolved in politics, but it does so at the cost of playing into existing stereotypes and giving the illusion of political participation. Whether that translates into offline participation in politics can only be discovered through empirical study of the activities of parody Web site users.

CONCLUSION

Mitra and Cohen (1999) argued that "the theoretical underpinnings of traditional analytic methods [for studying text] need to be rethought" (p. 199). This chapter has shown the truth of that statement by extending rhetorical theory to consider the strategic design of messages in clusters of text composed by groups of authors and designers who shared the same purpose and similar methods of appealing to their readers. What they needed was an audience of users who would visit (and hopefully revisit) their sites, tell their friends about them and send their URLs to other users, and make contributions or buy the products advertised on their sites.

By using an expanded concept of "text" as content that includes overall design, graphics, and strategic use of links, one can see how these authors kept readers on their sites and encouraged return visits. First, they established the background knowledge about candidate behavior and talk that could be parodied. Second, they began circulating a stable of commonplaces (ideas and examples used as discursive resources) that were readily recognizable to readers familiar with content on the cluster of sites. Third, they exploited these by constructing faux news reports, speeches, and stories composed for their readers' entertainment.

These rhetorical strategies worked well where more traditional strategies might fail because hypertext does not lend itself well to the linear development and logical forms of print media. Instead, one has to rely on networks of reciprocal links, intertextual allusions, and appeals to beliefs and attitudes presumably shared by site users. One has thus to appeal to a community of interest constructed through and by means of the text itself.

Site authors made their readers feel a part of this space by constructing an audience who was in the know and could appreciatively follow the moves of the parodic game. Through coined terms (e.g., "Dubya" for Bush), allusions (e.g., to "Pops" or "Big Daddy," for the senior Bush), and intertextual references (to "Slovakians" or "compassionate conservatism"), they appealed to readers already savvy about the discursive environment of these sites. These forms of intertextuality were intentional and explicit (Mitra, 1999). Rather than opening up the text by expanding the matrix of intertextual production, the intertextual allusions on these sites bound them together in a nested set of self reinforcing cross-references (Ott & Walter, 2000).

When compared with political parody sites in 1996, these 2000 sites were much more intentionally designed and strategically structured. The most successful among them carved out a textual space through interlaced patterns of reference and allusion, and they designed messages that developed progressively and produced a convergence of thought and ideology. Here many users could freely sample site content and be entertained, but they were likely to be persuaded at the same time.

Conclusion: Whom Does Technology Serve?

This book has examined communication on and about new media technology in an effort to learn more about how it affects our society, culture, and consciousness. The focus has been on clusters of sites on the World Wide Web and in general interest periodicals about communication technology. Because the Web is very large, I have focused on discourse practices in two topic areas—technology and politics. I selected these because studying them sheds light on some of the major questions raised by the potential of new media communication. To what extent and in what ways does it bring people together and foster community? Whose interests are served and whose are disadvantaged by new media development? What does politics on the Internet mean for the public interest? If life online is in any sense a mirror of culture, what does it tell us about our values and priorities as a society? These are big questions, and although these studies do not provide definitive answers, they do contribute to an ongoing discussion about such issues and complement survey research, which has been reported where it is relevant.

To answer such questions, I selected in each case a segment of discourse that was identifiable by virtue of its topic, its audiences, a time period, and an agenda. Chapter 1 examined the content of *Wired* magazine in the late 1990s and early 2000; chapter 2 considered discourse inviting women online from 1994 to 1997; and chapter 3 examined political parody Web sites in the 2000 presidential campaign and compared them with similar sites posted in 1996. By consistently identifying in these texts those features that were consciously or unconsciously used to design messages and adapt them to prospective audiences, I learned a great deal about how communication technologies are used and whose interests they serve.

DELIBERATION AND ITS ABSENCE

Chapters 1 and 2 studied a kind of civic discourse that has been called *technological elitism* (B. Fisher et al., 1996). The readership of *Wired* and the cybergrrls each functioned as "thin communities" (Bimber, 1998). To some extent, each group shared particular forms of knowledge, held complementary and common values, and was prepared to act collectively on matters of mutual concern. Their rhetorical strategies also revealed how the technological elite controls the discourse about technology and shapes public opinion.

Within the context of technology-oriented media coverage, technological elites have many resources at their disposal. First, they can draw on what Selfe (1999) called a "historically determined belief" (p. 115) among Americans in a grand narrative of technological progress within a capitalistic framework. Second, because they have the financial resources and media access to communicate their message, their views dominate in much of the media discourse about communication technology. Third, technological elites (as compared with the rest of us) share a certain mystique by virtue of their specialized forms of knowledge and expertise that others depend on.

Because of these rhetorical resources, technological elites were able to use discursive strategies unavailable to many other sectors of society. They could define the terms of the discussion by using dichotomies revealed in rhetorical dissociation (technologically savvy vs. Luddite, superconnected vs. unconnected, etc.). They coined terms (Digital Citizen, Netizen, cybergrrl) especially to describe their own unique attributes. They also selected certain individuals as models to be emulated, thereby elevating certain traits and suppressing others. Such forms of argument and language use enabled them to strengthen their own group identities as fearless, active innovators setting standards that others would follow.

The technological elite's "in the know" position enabled its members to use rhetorical strategies of exhortation and epideictic as well. Creating exigencies and a sense of urgency, some cybergrrls admonished their readers to get online or miss out on life's opportunities. *Wired's* writers often used narrative patterns in which the outcome of a narrative was foreordained and the steps leading to it were told as a flashback. In such narratives, events had their own momentum. Time was running out, and an individual's fate rested on relentless hard work and other forces beyond his or her control. These appeals and stories succeeded because they were predicated on a network of unquestioned assumptions held in common by consumers of the discourse who were drawn to it precisely because they shared its worldview.

The use of epideictic (speech that celebrates consensually held values) rather than deliberation (speech that critically examines issues) was in itself a problem in these case studies. Epideictic can only succeed in situations where its audience is inclined to be of one mind and disinclined to weigh opposing points of view or alternate courses of action. As Gurak (1997) observed:

> In any community of shared values, including the discretely divided electronic communities of newsgroups, mailing lists, and other cyberspaces, the model of free discussion is often composed of Athenians being praised in Athens.... [C]ommunities often become self-selecting and may not challenge the information they obtain in cyberspace forums. Instead, they choose to believe it because certain messages appeal to their shared values. (p. 85)

This is not an unusual phenomenon, nor is it unique to CMC but it was particularly pronounced among the groups of writers studied in chapters 1 and 2. Readers new to their discourse might be quite surprised to hear about certain ideas that were presented matter-of-factly; for example, plans to create a society in which certain groups are screened out, or a scenario in which human intelligence is completely eclipsed by artificial intelligence, or genesis of a "hive mind" used by all (technologically connected) people on the globe to act as one. That such ideas were put forward and presumably went unquestioned attests to the high level of consensus of *Wired*'s readership.

Of equal concern were the patterns of emphasis and neglect that emerged in the cybergrrl and *Wired* discourses. Technical astuteness, aggressiveness, affluence, and status were lauded, sought after, and elevated in importance as ends in themselves. Discussions of the needs of society's poor and disadvantaged were very rare, as were appeals to social consciousness. Some very questionable, if not illegal, practices were reported with little or no commentary. The posture was one of ethical ambivalence, and some readers might wonder what values, other than success and monetary profit, played a role in this discourse community.

Chapter 1 also presented ample evidence for *Wired*'s tendency to underreport the activities and accomplishments of women and certain ethnic groups. For example, our follow-up survey (a raw count of photo and article content in six 1999 and 2000 issues of the magazine) revealed that 87% of codable textual references were to men and 12% were to women. Of 470 photos in the six issues, 80% were of Whites, 7% were of African Americans, 14% were of Asians, and less than 1% were of Latinos. Furthermore, as descriptions of the writing about ethnic group members in chapter 1 indicate, there frequently was a tendency to exoticize, tokenize, or stigmatize them. Apologists for the magazine might maintain that these patterns were unintentional or the result of *Wired*'s writers' efforts to write for their largely White, male readership. However, such patterns do reflect an emphasis on entertainment and reinforcement of existing values and stereotypes. If the non-White population in the United States is to participate fully in the opportunities and benefits of new communication technologies and if the "digital divide" is to be closed, then deliberate efforts at greater inclusiveness are called for.

Chapter 3 on Web-based political parody extended and added to some of the work in earlier chapters. Although this chapter focused on a different sector of Internet activity (political communication), some of the same trends appeared. For example, messages posted on the parody sites showed that many visitors were attracted to them because of shared values and common interests. The type of civic life I found on these parody sites seemed to take the form of like-minded exchange in which participants avoided views discrepant from their own and sought out those with which they concurred. As B. Fisher et al. (1996) observed, this form of political participation can "reinforce the fragmentation and factionalism of modern society" (p. 14).

Studies of parody in both the 1996 and 2000 presidential campaigns showed that because of the Internet's capacity to exploit hypertext, it works very well as a platform for parody. Digitized photographs, plagiarized frames, composite candidates, and imported video and audio clips worked well to expose candidates' misstatements, equivocations, and gaffes. Parody sites were very entertaining and attracted younger users, but they were informative as well. The 2000 parody sites, in particular, took pains to document their allusions by embedding links to legitimate media articles about the real candidates' words and actions. On the other hand, the forms of interaction on the parody sites would do little to contribute to or influence the political process. Instead, visitors to these sites could play political computer games, respond to pseudo-polls, submit content to site Webmasters, and purchase various campaign artifacts. Like the cybergrrl sites in chapter 2, the parody sites were seemingly interactive because users could e-mail the Webmaster, post content to message boards, and write to pseudo-candidates, but much of this interactivity was simulated rather than actual.

These parody sites, taken together, functioned in mutual synchrony, coordinating their efforts in various ways. They bound themselves together through reciprocal links, intertextuality, use of coined terms, and lateral cross-references shared among sites. As a group, they constituted a discourse "community," but it was more an enclave of like-minded exchangers deriving pleasure from their positions as being "in the know" about candidates' past gaffes and misstatements.

The structure and textual features of discourse practices enacted in these case studies tell us many things about communication in Internet environments. Like other media sectors, the Internet can provide a platform for special interests and like-minded exchangers to establish group identities, support each other's views, and appeal to potential recruits and external constituencies. Such groups are not prone to deliberation or critical analysis, and they often do not serve the public interest. Because of the absence of controversy, alternative views, and open discussion, these venues do not encourage their audiences to think about the effects of technology on society. Instead, they foster self-interested individualism and inattention to major social and political issues.

Comparison of parody sites in 1996 and 2000 revealed the ways that the Internet, and the Web in particular, has become increasingly more commercialized and less egalitarian as it has grown and become more structured. Posting and maintaining a Web presence now appears to be more difficult than it was 5 years ago. Top-ranked sites that attract visitors and media attention require a great deal of time and effort. Required resources include a Web hosting service, professional site designers, inclusion on major search engines, and corporate sponsors. The Web is no longer a free and open place where anyone can put up a Web site and attract an audience. Although the Web continues to be a resource for social support and community activism, the hoped-for emergence of a Web-based public forum has not yet come to pass.

RHETORICAL RESPONSE: THE NEED FOR A COUNTERNARRATIVE

Those who call for critical scrutiny of protechnology discourse face a sizable rhetorical challenge. Many journalists and writers of books and trade periodicals tell a beguiling narrative. The optimists among them predict a bright future of unending economic prosperity, prolonged life, and startling advances in biotechnology and medicine. These spokesmen benefit from a strong protechnology bias in many public sectors, and their narratives and predictions are told and disseminated in media forums dominated by corporate interests highly vested in development of new communication and scientific technologies.

The problem faced by technology critics was succinctly described by Talbott (1995), who observed, "the problem we're up against ... is hard to put a dramatic name to. In fact this very difficulty partly defines the problem" (p. 33). This lack of a "dramatic name" alludes to the critics' failure to offer an alternative identity, an understandable counternarrative, or a set of metaphors that have public appeal. A problem similar to this was identified by Ivie (1987), who described the failure of Cold War "idealists" to dispel images of Soviet savagery and carve out a middle ground for public policy formation relevant to our Soviet foreign policy. Ivie explained that these idealists used self-defeating metaphors that placed guilt on the U.S. public, appealed to its fears, and offered unpalatable options to replace existing policy. Ivie concluded his analysis by observing that what was needed was a new set of metaphors that envisioned a sense of world stewardship and collaboration rather than the old savagery versus civilization cluster. A symbiotic metaphorical cluster, he argued, would provide a platform for rhetorical (and conceptual) transcendence and enable productive discussion of future scenarios.

In the pro- and antitechnology controversy, a similar solution might be called for. On the one side, protechnology advocates often resort to an unrelieved and uncritical enthusiasm that might well just be called hype. On the other side, their opponents seem to be working from a limited and largely unsuccessful rhetorical repertoire. This repertoire relies on a number of strategies that seem not to coalesce and to be ineffective because of their scattered nature and their generally negative valence. Technology critics' responses can be characterized as follows: dire prediction, nostalgia, silence, and rational argument. One possible reason for the first three of these responses might be that the cohort of skeptics is comprised of representatives of what Tapscott (1998) called the "old media" generation.

In describing the new generation of young people who have grown up with and embraced computer technology, Tapscott observed:

An old generation that is comfortable with its old communications media is being made uneasy by a new generation and a new communications media [sic] that is controlled by no one. For the first time, the new generation understands the new media much better and is embracing it much faster. (p. 50)

The problem for technology critics such as Talbott (1995) and S. E. Miller (1996) who issued dire predictions is that they are unable to project a vision of a future in which technology improves society. Instead, they see a future in which the illiterate, underprivileged, and undertechnologized will become ever more oppressed. At times, they also consider a future in which runaway technology development gets accepted and adopted merely because it is being developed and marketed. The effects of these developments are worker displacement and loss of know-how. These effects can be combined with the increasing corporatization of governments. The resulting loss of public accountability and knowing who is responsible would lead to a society in which no one identifiable is protecting the public interest. What is envisioned, then, is an Orwellian society and loss of faith in democratic government.

Another response taken by technology critics is nostalgia, which, although it might appeal effectively to members of the print culture, is not geared to the interests or values of the new media generation. Nowhere is this more apparent than in nostalgia for the card catalog and the traditional library, but it can also be seen in anxiety about what will happen to the book as a cultural artifact. Other forms of nostalgia often accompany the one for print. One takes the form of regret for loss of that *arete* that comprised true literacy—knowledge of history, literature, composition, and grammar—that new technologies such as spell checkers, grammar checkers, translation programs, outliners, and documentation programs so readily supply. Another is concern about the potential loss of experiential, geographically proximate "real" communities. Although reminiscences about life before the Internet and complaints about the quality of Internet-based communication have merit, they do not have a great deal of meaning for young people who thrive on e-mail, chat, and cell phone conversation.

Another form of nostalgia is for face-to-face communication and is due to an underlying fear that new technologies bring with them increasing social isolation and detachment from interest in political activity. Talbott (1995) worried that new communications technologies would lead to a decline in the richness of discourse, barren abstractness, and mutual alienation. Turkle (1995) noted that "many of the institutions that used to bring people together—a main street, a union hall, a town meeting—no longer work as before. Many people spend most of their day alone at the screen of a television or a computer" (p. 177). These concerns, and the already-developing nostalgia for in-person human contact, are echoed in the work of Doheny-Farina (1996) and Brook and Boal (1995).

A third kind of response (it would be a misnomer to label it a strategy) is silence. The old media generation harbors many fears. These include fears of becoming obsolete, fears of technology itself, and fears of the loss of print culture. Instead of openly addressing these fears, many technoskeptics say nothing about them. This absence is problematic, for the old media readership needs, perhaps more than any other group, to be reassured. They need to be reminded that sometimes even expert computer scientists cannot configure a laptop to perform the functions they need; that appropriate prophylactic measures and backups can safeguard one's work, protecting it from viruses and erasure; and that hypermedia do not contribute to the loss of literacy but to a new kind of literacy (Tapscott, 1998). It could be that silence on these issues only exacerbates the fears harbored by many readers and leads to a lack of open discussion on issues vital to adoption of new communications technologies.

The final strategy used by skeptics is rational argument. Exemplars of this approach include Haraway (1997), S. E. Miller (1996), and Rochlin (1997). Their analyses are thought provoking and insightful, and they exemplify the sort of stimuli that could lead to meaningful public deliberation about the impact of new technologies on society. Haraway examined how knowledge, particularly knowledge about new biomedical technology, is rhetorically constructed. Her incisive analysis reveals the many ways in which we are already becoming cyborgs—amalgams produced by reproductive technologies, genetic engineering, and computer-mediated representations. S. E. Miller examined the implications of new communications technologies for free speech, surveillance, privacy, diversity, and economic development in contemporary society. Rochlin looked specifically at the impact of new technologies on the material conditions of our lives—the conduct of war, airline safety, and stock market fluctuation. His findings are chilling reminders of what can happen when technology goes wrong. The only rhetorical difficulty with these authors' sound appraisals is that they are not coordinated and, because they offer no counternarrative, they do not capture the public imagination.

An examination of present circumstances, however, implies that a counternarrative to the libertarian ideology (discussed in chapter 1) is very much needed. The only narrative around which any consensus has formed to date is that of the libertarians who believe that the public interest is best served by letting the free market take its course. The libertarian optimism that holds that market interests and private philanthropy will address the relentlessly growing income and technology gaps in this country and throughout the world is belied by fact. Recent figures indicate that the richest 1% (2.7 million) of U.S. families have as many after-tax dollars to spend as the bottom 100 million and that the poorest one fifth of households averaged $8,800 of income in 1999, down from $10,000 in 1977. Because of the cumulative effect of tax cuts since 1977 and other factors, the rich are getting richer and the poor are getting poorer (Johnston, 1999). It is also the case that Internet use is predominantly Caucasian (over 80% White), and minorities comprise a decided minority of Internet participation (approximately 15% for all groups taken together; Jordan, 1999). Because the liber-

tarian narratives about a level playing field, flattened hierarchies, and equal opportunity to participate for all groups seem
to be false, any rhetorically effective counternarrative would
need to be more sensitive to the facts of the matter.

A rhetorical middle course must be steered between uncritical enthusiasm for new technologies and bleak rejection of
them. Uncritical enthusiasm encourages unthinking accep-
tance, whereas bleak rejection paints a picture that is doomed
to be rejected by the public. Intelligent discussion of issues related to Internet policy is what is needed. Fortunately, forums
do exist for such discussion; one problem may be that they have
not yet gotten as much coverage in the popular media as they
should, and consequently, their work has not been made salient
in public awareness about technology issues.

Forums on Internet policy include such organizations as the
Electronic Frontier Foundation, Computer Professionals for Social Responsibility, the Institute for Social Assessment of Information Technology, the Internet Policy Institute, and People for
Internet Responsibility. The Electronic Frontier Foundation
(www.eff.org) is a nonprofit, nonpartisan group whose aim is to
increase public understanding of Internet-related issues, raise
public awareness about civil liberties, and contribute to
policymakers' understanding of the need for open, free telecom-
munication. Computer Professionals for Social Responsibility
(www.cpsr.org) is made up of computer scientists and technical
experts who are well qualified to advise the public and
policymakers on issues related to Internet governance, voting
and election technology, and free speech and intellectual property. This group works to dispel popular myths about the infalli-
bility of technological systems and challenges that idea that
technology alone can solve social problems. The Institute for Social Assessment of Information Technology (www.isait.vt.edu)
studies the role of informatics in various sectors of society, and it
also identifies and evaluates the potential social consequences of
future information technologies.

The two remaining organizations are specifically dedicated to
promoting public discussion and deliberation about Internet pol-

icy. The first, the Internet Policy Institute (www.internetpolicy. org), is an independent research institute with the aim of providing high-quality analysis, education, and outreach on technology policy. It has endeavored to help various corporate and academic communities organize debates and discussions. In 2000, it supported a series of town hall meetings throughout the country in an effort to gather public input on Internet policy. The second, People for Internet Responsibility (www.pfir.org), is a global network of individuals interested in Internet policy and regulation. Its aim is to gather input and encourage reasonable discussion of Internet policy issues.

The conversation that is underway will inevitably entail values and value choices, but it is also based on research about technology's effects. There has been far too much media hype about technology development and far too little reasoned discussion and debate based on empirical research of its actual effects. Does the Internet enhance or undermine interest in politics and political deliberation? How does instructional technology improve or change student learning? What measures could be used to promote greater use of technology by society's underprivileged groups? How are people being hurt, and how significantly, by dissemination of health and credit information made possible by technology? When new technologies are developed, how do they extend or amend the circumstances relevant to issues such as these?

Well-crafted policy concerning new communication technologies will depend on public awareness of the stakes involved in decisions about regulation of new media. However, information alone is not enough. The depth of public thought will grow out of reasoned public advocacy that contemplates issues such as access, privacy, censorship, economic impacts, and social isolation. We can anticipate a promising future enabled by new technology only when the public thoroughly understands all the alternatives available and the means of choosing between them. For their choices to be informed choices, media audiences must be made aware of the ways in which much media coverage of technology issues carries a protechnology bias.

Through rhetorical analysis, this book has uncovered some of the underlying myths, narratives, stereotypes, assumptions, and forms of argument that have colored public understanding of the issues involved in the development of communication technology. If all media representations are constructions, then a clear understanding of their design can contribute to critical literacy on technology issues. A public that is fully aware of how they are persuaded to adopt certain views of technology will be prepared to shape Internet policy in the future.

References

About us. (1999). *Wired* [Online]. Retrieved August 25, 1999 from the World Wide Web: http://www.wired.com/wired/about/

algore-2000.org. (2000). Welcome to algore-2000.org! Retrieved July 22, 2000 from the World Wide Web: http://www.algore-2000.org/

All Gore. (2000). All Gore briefing room: Announcement of partnership to decorate one million homes, Friday, June 11, 1999. Retrieved July 22, 2000 from the World Wide Web: http://www.allgore.com/release04.shtml

Allis, S. (2000, April 16). I, robot will self-replicating robots rule us? Will we become hybrids, part human and part machine? Such questions no longer come only from fanatics and fearmongers. *The Boston Globe* [Online]. Available Lexis-Nexis Job Number 59:0:14797074

Althusser, L. (1972). Ideology and ideological state apparatuses (Notes towards an investigation). In B. Brewster (Trans.), *Lenin and philosophy, and other essays* (pp. 127–186). New York: Monthly Review Press.

Astor, G. (1996, April). Computer marriage: The mouse that roared. *Cosmopolitan, 220*(4), 218.

Bakhtin, M. M (1981). *The dialogic imagination* (C. Emerson & M. Holquist, Trans.). Austin: University of Texas Press.

Bayers, C. (1998, November). Mike Homer's guide to professional success. *Wired, 7.10,* 158–161, 216, 218, 220–221.

Bayers, C. (1999, December). Code warrior. *Wired, 7.12,* 160, 162, 166, 168, 170.

Beato, G. (1997, April). Girl games. *Wired, 5.04* [Online]. Retrieved August 7, 1997 from the World Wide Web: http://www.wired.com/5.04/girlgames/ff_girlgames.html

Bellah, R. N., Madsen, R., Sullivan, W. M., Swidler, A., & Tipton, S. M. (1996). *Habits of the heart: Individualism and commitment in American life* (Rev. ed.). Berkeley: University of California Press.

Bennahum, D. S. (1997, November). Heart of darkness. *Wired, 5.11,* 226–230, 266, 268, 270, 272, 274, 276.

Bennahum, D. S. (1998, September). When we were young. *Wired, 6.09,* 128–129, 190–191.

Berland, J. (2000). Cultural technologies and the "evolution" of technological cultures. In A. Herman & T. Swiss (Eds.), *The World Wide Web and contemporary cultural theory* (pp. 235–258). New York: Routledge.

129

Bimber, B. (1998). The Internet and political transformation: Populism, community, and accelerated pluralism. *Polity, 31,* 133–160. Retrieved July 17, 2000 from the World Wide Web: www.polsci.ucsb.edu/faculty/bimber/research/transformation.html

Bitzer, L. F. (1968). The rhetorical situation. *Philosophy and Rhetoric, 1,* 1–14.

Bizzell, P., & Herzberg, B. (Eds.). (1990). *The rhetorical tradition.* Boston: St. Martin's.

Bolter, J. D., & Grusin, R. (1999). *Remediation: Understanding new media.* Cambridge, MA: MIT Press.

Borsook, P. (1996). The memoirs of a token: An aging Berkeley feminist examines *Wired.* In L. Cherny & E. R. Weise (Eds.), *Wired women: Gender and new realities in cyberspace* (pp. 24–41). Seattle, WA: Seal Press.

Bradley-gore2000.com. (2000). Ask Al. Retrieved July 21, 2000 from the World Wide Web: www.bradley-gore2000.com/BradleyGore/viewer%20Mail.htm

Brame, G. G. (1996, June). Seismic shifts: How technology will change the way you work. *Working Woman, 21*(6), 30–33.

Brockman, J. (1996). *Digerati: Encounters with the cyber elite.* San Francisco: HardWired.

Bronson, P. (1999, July). GenEquity. *Wired, 7.07,* 112–123, 168, 171–172, 174–180.

Brook, J., & Boal, I. A. (Eds.). (1995). *Resisting the virtual life: The culture and politics of information.* San Francisco: City Lights.

BSNN.net. (1999, April 14). Ventura tops Gore's VP wish list. Retrieved August 2, 2000 from the World Wide Web: http://www.bsnn.net/JesseGore.htm

Burke, K. (1950). *A rhetoric of motives.* Berkeley: University of California Press.

Burke, K. (1966). *Language as symbolic action: Essays on life, literature, and method.* Berkeley: University of California Press.

Bush for President, Inc. (2000). Governor Bush welcomes you to his virtual campaign headquarters. Retrieved July 21, 2000 from the World Wide Web: http://www.georgewbush.com

Butler, J. (1997). *The psychic life of power: Theories in subjection.* Stanford: Stanford University Press.

Cambridge Dictionaries Online. (2000). Parody. Retrieved July 18, 2000 from the World Wide Web: dictionary. Cambridge.org

Case, D. (1997, November). Big brother is alive and well in Vietnam—And he really hates the Web. *Wired, 5.11,* 164, 166, 168, 173, 175–176.

Castells, M. (1996). *The rise of the network society.* Malden, MA: Blackwell.

Chesebro, J. W., & Bertelsen, D. A. (1996). *Analyzing media: Communication technologies as symbolic and cognitive systems.* New York: Guilford.

Chesebro, J. W., & Bonsell, D. G. (1989). *Computer-mediated communication: Human relationships in a computerized world.* Tuscaloosa: University of Alabama Press.

Coover, R. (1992, June 21). The end of books. *The New York Times Book Review,* 1, 23–25. Abstract available: http://web3.infotrac.galegroup.com/itw/infomark/174/158/37121975w3/purl=rcl_EAIM_0_A12275628&dyn=3!xr n_15_0_A12275628&bkm_3_15?sw_aep=wash_eai

Davis, R. (1999). *The web of politics: The Internet's impact on the American political system.* New York: Oxford University Press.

Dawson, M., & Foster, J. B. (1998). Virtual capitalism. In R. W. McChesney, E. M. Wood, & J. B. Foster (Eds.), *Capitalism and the information age* (pp. 51–67). New York: Monthly Review Press.

DeLoach, A. (1996, March 1). Grrls exude attitude. *CMC Magazine* [Online serial]. Retrieved August 7, 1997 from the World Wide Web: www.december.com/cmc/mag/1996/mar/deloach.html

Dertouzos, M. L. (1999, August). The future of computing. *Scientific American, 281,* 52–55.

DieTryin.com. (2000). Remarks by Governor Bush Lite, June 12, 1999. Retrieved July 7, 2000 from the World Wide Web: http://www.bushlite.net/speech.html

Doheny-Farina, S. (1996). *The wired neighborhood.* New Haven, CT: Yale University Press.

Edwards, J. (2000, March). Rants and raves [Letter to editor]. *Wired, 8.03,* 69.

Election.com, Inc. (2000). Minority vote in Arizona Presidential preference primary strengthened by high voter turnout. Retrieved June 23, 2000 from the World Wide Web: http://www.election.com/pressroom/pr2000/0324.htm

Exley, Z. (1999). Letter to Lawrence M. Noble, esq., General Counsel, Federal Election Commission. Retrieved August 20, 2000 from the World Wide Web: http://www.gwbush.com/meteofec/htm

Fisher, B., Margolis, M., & Resnick, D. (1996). Breaking ground on the virtual frontier: Surveying civic life on the Internet. *American Sociologist, 27,* 11–29.

Fisher, W. R. (1987). *Human communication as narration: Toward a philosophy of reason, value, and action.* Columbia: University of South Carolina Press.

Fost, D. (1999, June 7). Under Condé Nast, magazine has boosted fortune by focusing on "new economy." *The San Francisco Chronicle,* p. E1. [Online]. Available Lexis-Nexis.

Fraser, N. (1989). *Unruly practices: Power, discourse, and gender in contemporary social theory.* Minneapolis: University of Minnesota Press.

Frauenfelder, M. (1999, October). The back-door director. *Wired, 7.10,* 236–245.

Freund, J. (1997, September). Chip hop: What happens when the hood meets cyberspace? *Wired, 5.09,* 148–153, 197–198, 207.

Friedman, T. (1995). Making sense of software: Computer games and interactive textuality. In S. G. Jones (Ed.), *Cybersociety: Computer-mediated communication and community* (pp. 78–89). Thousand Oaks, CA: Sage.

Fryer, B. (1997, March). The next Bill Gates? *Working Woman, 22*(3), 34–37, 87.

Gallup Organization. (2000). *Gallup Poll Surveys: February 20–21, 2000.* Retrieved June 21, 2000 from the World Wide Web: http://www.gallup.com/poll/surveys/2000/topline000220/q10t27.asp

Gates, B. (1995). *The Road Ahead* with N. Myhrvold & P. Rhineasun. New York: Viking.

George Washington University Graduate School of Political Management. (2000a). *Characteristics of 1998 campaign Web sites.* Retrieved June 28, 2000 from the World Wide Web: http://democracyonline.org/databank/sites98.shtml

George Washington University Graduate School of Political Management. (2000b). *Executive summary: Democracy online survey December 6, 1999.* Retrieved June 28, 2000 from the World Wide Web: http://democracyonline.org/databank/dec6survey.shtml

Gibson, W. (1984). *Neuromancer.* New York: Ace.

Glassman, J. (1995, August). The infinite possibilities of going online. *Cosmopolitan, 219*(2), 124.

Goetz, T. (1997, August 5). Trip wired: Another digital revolution meets reality. *The Village Voice,* p. 31. [Online]. Lexis-Nexis.

Gore 2000. (2000). Remarks as prepared for delivery by Vice President Gore, Tuesday, May 2, 2000—Atlanta, GA. Retrieved July 31, 2000 from the World Wide Web: http://www.algore2000.com/speeches/ sp_05022000_ga.html

Graphics, Visualization, and Usability Center. (1995). *GVUs 3rd WWW user survey* [Online]. Atlanta: College of Computing, Georgia Institute of Technology. Retrieved August 18, 1997 from the World Wide Web: http://www.gvu. gatech.edu/user_surveys/survey-04-1995

Graphics, Visualization, and Usability Center. (1997). *GVUs 8th WWW user survey.* [Online]. Atlanta: College of Computing, Georgia Institute of Technology. Retrieved January 20, 1998 from the World Wide Web: http://www.gvu. gatech.edu/user_surveys/survey-1997-10

Group publishers' 2000-versus-1999 ad page review (2001, February 12). [Online]. *Min Media Industry Newsletter, 54*(7). Lexis-Nexis.

Gurak, L. J. (1997). *Persuasion and privacy in cyberspace: The online protests over Lotus MarketPlace and the clipper chip.* New Haven, CT: Yale University Press.

Gurak, L. J. (2001). *Cyberliteracy: Navigating the Internet with awareness.* New Haven, CT: Yale University Press.

gwbush.com. (2000). GWBush.com is winning on the issues. Retrieved August 25, 2000 from the World Wide Web: http://www.gwbush.com

Haraway, D. (1997). *Modest_witness@Second_millennium: Femaleman©_meets_ Oncomouse^{TM}.* New York: Routledge.

Harris Interactive. (1999, December 22). *Harris Poll #76: Online population growth surges to 56% of all adults.* New York: Creators Syndicate. Retrieved July 1, 2000 from the World Wide Web: http://www.harrisinteractive.com

Heron, K. (1998, July). Original spin: Why Gore Vidal shorts the future. *Wired, 6.07,* 130–131.

Herring, S. (1994, June 27). *Gender differences in computer-mediated communication: Bringing familiar baggage to the new frontier.* Paper presented at the convention of the American Library Association, Miami, FL. Retrieved August 7, 1997 from the World Wide Web: www.cpsr.org/gender/herring.txt

Hobbs, R. (1998). The seven great debates in the media literacy movement. *Journal of Communication, 48,* 16–32.

Howe, P. J. (2001, March 13). Techs steer Wall Street into a big, wide pothole. *Seattle Post-Intelligencer,* pp. A1, A5.

Hudes, K. (1998, October 19). 'Wired's' elitist futurism now grounded in the reality of readers Condé Nast brings 'support' rather than 'direction' to techtitle, *Advertising Age,* p. S6 [Online]. Available Lexis-Nexis.

Hudson, D. (1997). *Rewired.* Indianapolis, IN: Macmillan.

Ignatius, D. (2000, May 17). The new Frankenstein. *The Washington Post* [Online]. Lexis-Nexis Job Number 711:0:14796974

It's a bitch being rich. (1999). *Wired, 7.09, 76.*

Ivie, R. L. (1987). Metaphor and the rhetorical invention of cold war "idealists." *Communication Monographs, 54,* 165–182.

Jamieson, K. H. (1992). *Dirty politics: Deception, distraction, and democracy.* New York: Oxford University Press.

Jamieson, K. H. (2000). *Everything you think you know about politics ... and why you're wrong.* New York: Basic Books.

Johns, A. (1999). Philanthropic pop. *Wired, 7.07,* 148–149.

Johnston, D. C. (1999, September 5). Rich get richer as most people share less of pie, report says. *Seattle Times,* pp. A1, A22.

Jordan, T. (1999). *Cyberpower: The culture and politics of cyberspace and the Internet.* London: Routledge.

Joy, B. (2000, April). Why the future doesn't need us. *Wired, 8.04,* 238–245, 248–263.

Kantrowitz, B. (1994, May 16). Men, women, and computers. *Newsweek, 123,* 48–55.

Katz, J. (1995, September). Guilty. *Wired, 3.09,* 128–133, 188.

Katz, J. (1997, December). The digital citizen. *Wired, 5.12,* 68–69, 71–72, 76, 78, 80, 82, 274–275.

Kelly, K. (1999, September). The roaring zeros. *Wired, 7.09,* 150–155.

Kelly, K., & Reiss, S. (1998, August). One huge computer. *Wired, 6.08,* 128–133, 168–170.

Kennedy, G. (1963). *The art of persuasion in Greece.* Princeton, NJ: Princeton University Press.

Kennedy, G. A. (1991). *Aristotle on rhetoric.* New York: Oxford University Press.

Kennedy, H., & Siemaszko, C. (2000, February 19). Malapropism thing runs in Bush family. *New York Daily News.* Retrieved August 2, 2000 from the World Wide Web: http://www.nydailynews.com/2002-02-19/News_and_Views/Beyond_the_City/a-57365.asp

Kenner, R. (1999, October). My Hollywood! *Wired, 7.10,* 217–221.

Kirsner, S. (1999, September). Nonprofit motive. *Wired, 7.09,* 110, 112, 114–116, 118.

Kirsner, S. (2000, February). All the news that's fit to pixel. *Wired, 8.02,* 126, 128, 130, 132, 134–135, 138, 141–142.

Kubey, R. (1998). Obstacles to the development of media education in the U. S. *Journal of Communication, 48,* 58–69.

Kurzweil, R. (1999). *The age of spiritual machines: When computers exceed human intelligence.* New York: Viking.

Ladd, D. (1996, June). Move over boys: Net chicks are here to stay. *Peak Computing* [Online serial]. Retrieved August 7, 1997 from the World Wide Web: www.peak-computing.com/96/jun/07/feature.html

Landow, G. P. (1997). *Hypertext 2.0: The convergence of contemporary critical theory and technology.* Baltimore: Johns Hopkins.

Lanham, R. A. (1993). *The electronic word: Democracy, technology, and the arts.* Chicago: University of Chicago Press.

Lazarus, D. (1997, November). Death of Minitel. *Wired, 5.11,* 54.

Lehman, P. D. (1999, November). Blast from the past. *Wired, 7.11,* 200, 202, 204, 206, 208, 212, 214, 216, 218, 220–222, 224.

Leonard, A. (2000, January). As the MEMS revolution takes off, small is getting bigger every day. *Wired, 8.01,* 162, 164.

Leslie, J. (1999, November). Operation Phnom.com. *Wired, 7.11,* 230, 232, 234, 236, 238, 240, 242, 244, 246, 248, 250, 252, 254.

Lester, W. (2000, July 4). Truth be told, we're looking for honest candidates. *Seattle Post-Intelligencer,* p. A3.

Light, J. S. (1995). The digital landscape: New space for women? *Gender, Place, and Culture, 2,* 133–146.

Lohr, S. (1995, September 27). Who uses the Internet? *The New York Times,* p. D2.

Maloney, J. (1998, March–April). Why Wired misfired. *Columbia Journalism Review, 36,* 10(2) [Online]. Retrieved July 5, 1999 from the World Wide Web: http://web3.infotrac.galegroup.com, Article 20426237

Mantovani, G. (1996). *New communication environments: From everyday to virtual.* London: Taylor & Francis.

Marvin, C. (1987). *When old technologies were new.* New York: Oxford University Press.

Mays, J. (1997, May). Roaches in the machine. *Wired, 5.05* [Online]. Retrieved August 23, 1999 from the World Wide Web: http://www.wired.com/wired/archive/5.05/scans.html

McChesney, R. W. (1999). *Rich media, poor democracy: Communication politics in dubious times.* Urbana: University of Illinois Press.

Merkle, R. (2000, April 1). Blocking nanotechnology research: Not a good strategy. In *Will Spiritual Robots Replace Humanity by 2100?* Symposium supported by the Symbolic Systems Program, Stanford University. Transcript retrieved May 19, 2001 from the World Wide Web: http://www.technercast.com/tnc_program.html?program_id=82

Michals, D. (1997, March–April). Cyber-rape: How virtual is it? *Ms., 7,* 68–72.

Millar, M. S. (1998). *Cracking the gender code: Who rules the wired world?* Toronto: Second Story Press.

Miller, C. R. (1994). Opportunity, opportunism, and progress: *Kairos* in the rhetoric of technology. *Argumentation, 8,* 81–96.

Miller, L. (1995). Women and children first: Gender and the settling of the electronic frontier. In J. Brook & I. A. Boal (Eds.), *Resisting the virtual life: The culture and politics of information* (pp. 49–57). San Francisco: City Lights.

Miller, S. E. (1996). *Civilizing cyberspace: Policy, power, and the information superhighway.* New York: Addison-Wesley.

Minx manifesto. (1998). Retrieved January 6, 1998 from the World Wide Web: www.minxmag.com/index2.html

Mitra, A. (1999). Characteristics of the WWW text: Tracing discursive strategies. *Journal of Computer-Mediated Communication, 5* [Online serial]. Retrieved August 18, 2000 from the World Wide Web: http://www.ascusc.org/jcmc/vol5/issue1/mitra.html

Mitra, A., & Cohen, E. (1999). Analyzing the Web: Directions and challenges. In S. Jones (Ed.), *Doing Internet research: Critical issues and methods for examining the Net* (pp. 179–202). Thousand Oaks, CA: Sage.

Moran, S. (1998, May 18). Wired looks for a niche in a world it once defined. *Internet World* [Online]. Lexis-Nexis.

Morgan, J. (1995, April). Adventures in cyberspace. *Essence, 25*(4), 75.

Morgan, T. E. (1985). Is there an intertext in this class? Literary and interdisciplinary approaches to intertextuality. *American Journal of Semiotics, 3*, 1–40.

Nakayama, T. K., & Krizek, R. L. (1995). Whiteness: A strategic rhetoric. *Quarterly Journal of Speech, 81*, 291–309.

Neal, T. M. (1999, November 29). Satirical web site poses political test. *Washington Post* [Online]. Retrieved August 20, 2000 from the World Wide Web: http://www.washingtonpost.com/wp-dyn/articles/A55918-1999Nov28.html

Negroponte, N. (1998). Contraintuitive. *Wired, 6.08*, 184.

New London Group. (1996). A pedagogy of multiliteracies: Designing social futures. *Harvard Educational Review, 66*, 60–92.

Nicholas, R. (1995, September 5). World wide women. *Marketing*, 28.

Nie, N. H., & Erbring, L. (2000). *Internet and society: A preliminary report.* Stanford, CA: Stanford Institute for the Quantitative Study of Society. Retrieved June 26, 2000 from the World Wide Web: http://www.stanford.edu/group/siqss/Press_Release/internetStudy.html

Notess, G. R. (2000). *Search engine showdown: The users' guide to web searching.* Retrieved July 7, 2000 from the World Wide Web: searchengineshowdown.com/

Nua Ltd. (2000). *"How many online?"* New York: Nua Internet Surveys. Retrieved September 15, 2000 from the World Wide Web: http://www.nua.ie/surveys/how_many_online/index.html

Ogilvy, J. (1998, November). Dark side of the boom. *Wired, 6.11*, 188–189.

Olbrechts-Tyteca, L. (1979). Les couples philosophiques [Philosophical pairs]. *Revue Internationale de Philosophie, 127–128*, 81–98.

Ong, W. J. (1982). *Orality and literacy: The technologizing of the word.* London: Methuen.

Opportunities with Amazon City. (1998). Retrieved January 5, 1998 from the World Wide Web: www.amazoncity.com/cafe/

Ott, B. L.., & Walter, C. (2000). Intertextuality: Interpretive practice and textual strategy. *Critical Studies in Media Communication, 17*, 429–446.

Parks, B. (1999a, October). Anatomy of a spam. *Wired, 7.10*, 144, 146–148, 150, 152, 154, 156–158, 160, 164, 166.

Parks, B. (1999b, October). Independence day. *Wired, 7.10*, 222–224.

Paulsen, K. (1998, August). The Y2K solution: Run for your life! *Wired, 6.08*, 122–125, 164–167.

Penn, S. (1997). *The women's guide to the wired world: A user-friendly handbook and resource directory.* New York: The Feminist Press.

Perelman, C., & Olbrechts-Tyteca, L. (1969). *The new rhetoric: A treatise on argumentation* (J. Wilkinson & P. Weaver, Trans.). Notre Dame, IN: University of Notre Dame Press.

Pew Research Center for People and the Press. (1998). *Online newcomers more middlebrow, less work-oriented: The Internet news audience goes ordinary.* Retrieved June 28, 2000 from the World Wide Web: http://www.people-press.org/tech98que.htm

Platt, C. (1999a, December). The 38-gigahertz breakthrough. *Wired, 7.12,* 360–365.

Platt, C. (1999b, September). What's the big idea? *Wired, 7.09,* 122, 124, 126, 128–132.

Platt, C. (1999c, November). You've got smell. *Wired, 7.11,* 256–263.

Purdy, J. S. (1998, March–April). The God of the digerati. *The American Prospect, 37*(5), 86.

Resnick, D. (1997). Politics on the Internet: The normalization of cyberspace. *New Political Science, 41–42,* 47–67.

Rheingold, H. (1993). *The virtual community: Homesteading on the electronic frontier.* New York: HarperPerennial.

Rheingold, H. (1999, January). Look who's talking. *Wired, 7.01,* 128–131, 160–163.

Richardson, A. (1996). Come on, join the conversation!: 'Zines as a medium for feminist dialogue and community building. *Feminist Collections, 17* [Online]. Retrieved January 4, 1998 from the World Wide Web: www.library.wisc.edu/libraries/Women Studies/fcrichard.htm

Ricoeur, P. (1984). *Time and narrative: Vol. I* (K. McLaughlin & D. Pellauer, Trans.). Chicago: University of Chicago Press. (Original work published 1983)

Ritsch, M. (2000, April 23). Parody web sites skewer campaigns. *Los Angeles Times* [Online]. Retrieved August 20, 2000 from the World Wide Web: http:www.latimes.com/cgi-bin/print.cgi

Roach, M. (1999, December). Cute, Inc. *Wired, 7.12,* 332–338, 340–343.

Rochlin, G. I. (1997). *Trapped in the Net: The unanticipated consequences of computerization.* Princeton, NJ: Princeton University Press.

Rodino, M. (1997). Breaking out of binaries: Reconceptualizing gender and its relationship to language in computer-mediated communication. *Journal of Computer-Mediated Communication, 3* [Online serial]. Retrieved January 10, 1998 from the World Wide Web: jcmc.huji.ac.il/vol3/issue 3/rodino.html

Rossetto, L. (n.d.). *Response to the Californian ideology.* Retrieved August 8, 1999 from the World Wide Web: http://www.wmin.ac.uk/media/HRC/ci/calif2.html

Schlosser-Hall, C. C. (1996, November). *Global capitalism in technostyle: Constituting the digital generation in Wired magazine.* Paper presented at the annual meeting of the Speech Communication Association, San Diego, CA.

Schuyler, N., & Barad, V. (1996, June). It's not just e-male. *Working Woman, 21*(6), 38–43.

Schwartz, E. I. (1997). It's not retail! *Wired, 5.11,* 219–223, 287, 294.

Schwartz, J. (1996, March). An insider's guide to the Internet. *Working Woman, 21*(3), 49–52.

Segell, M. (1997, May). "I was raped by a man I met on the Internet."*Cosmopolitan, 222*(5), 146–148.

Selfe, C. L. (1999). *Technology and literacy in the twenty-first century: The importance of paying attention.* Carbondale: Southern Illinois University Press.

Sheff, D. (1999, November). Sony's plan for world recreation. *Wired, 7.11,* 264–269, 272–275.

Sherman, A. (1995, July–August). Claiming cyberspace: Five myths that are keeping women offline. *Ms., 6,* 26–28.

Sherman, A. (1997a, July 7). Are you a girl, grrl, gurl, grrrl, or what? *Cybergrrl Webstation* [Online]. Retrieved August 9, 1997 from the World Wide Web: www.cybergrrl/com/planet/sez/index7.html

Sherman, A. (1997b, July 7). Can girls be geeks too? *Cybergrrl Webstation* [Online]. Retrieved August 9, 1997 from the World Wide Web: www.cybergrrl.com/planet/sez/index8.html

Sherman, A. (1997c, December 3). Excuse Number 107: Computers are bad for you. *Cybergrrl Webstation* [Online]. Retrieved January 14, 1998 from the World Wide Web: www.cybergrrl.com/planet/sez/index 26.html

Sherman, A. (1998). Online advertising and sponsorships. *Cybergrrl, Inc.* [Online]. Retrieved January 14, 1998 from the World Wide Web: www.cgim.com/ad.html

Shogren, L. (2000, February 10). Candidates' efforts clicking on the Net. *Los Angeles Times,* p. A20.

Simons, J. (1996, October 21). Tired: Hyped firms Wired: Real profits. *U. S. News & World Report,* 68 [Online]. Lexis-Nexis.

Sinclair, C. (1996). *Net chick.* New York: Holt.

Sterling, B. (1998, July). The spirit of mega. *Wired, 6.07,* 106–122, 162–165.

Sterling, B. (2000, January). Newer York, New York. *Wired, 8.01,* 90, 92, 96, 98.

Stone, A. R. (1995). *The war of desire and technology at the close of the mechanical age.* Cambridge, MA: MIT Press.

Stross, R. E. (2000, April 3). Silicon Valley killjoy. *U. S. News Online.* Retrieved October 6, 2000 from the World Wide Web: http://www.usnews.com/usnews/issue/000403/tech.htm

Sutton, L. A. (1996). Cocktails and thumb tacks in the old West: What would Emily Post say? In L. Cherny & E. R. Weise (Eds.), *Wired women: Gender and new realities in cyberspace* (pp. 169–187). Seattle, WA: Seal Press.

Symbolic Systems Program. (2000). *Will spiritual robots replace humanity by 2100?* Retrieved October 15, 2000 from the World Wide Web. http://www.stanford.edu/dept/symbol/Hofstadter-event.html

Taggart, S. (1999, October). The 20-ton packet. *Wired, 7.10,* 246–255.

Talbott, S. L. (1995). *The future does not compute: Transcending the machines in our midst.* Sebastopol, CA: O'Reilly & Associates.

Tapscott, D. (1998). *Growing up digital: The rise of the net generation.* New York: McGraw-Hill.

Tetzlaff, D. (2000). Yo-ho-ho and a server of warez: Internet software piracy and the new global information economy. In A. Herman & T. Swiss (Eds.), *The World Wide Web and contemporary cultural theory* (pp. 99–126). New York: Routledge.

Thomas, S. G. (1997, March). The web: A complete women's guide. *Glamour, 95,* 248–251.

Travis, M. A. (1996, December). Cybernetic esthetics, hypertext, and the future of literature. *Mosaic: A Journal for the Interdisciplinary Study of Literature, 29* [Online]. Retrieved May 20, 2001 from the World Wide Web: Available Proquest: http://proquest.umi.com/pqdweb?ReqType=301&UserId=IPAuot&Passwd =IPAuto&COPT=REJTPTEwMzgrMTAyQSsxMjjG&JSEnabled=1&TS=990 370721

Turkle, S. (1984). *The second self: Computers and the human spirit.* New York: Simon & Schuster.

Turkle, S. (1995). *Life on the screen: Identity in the age of the Internet.* New York: Simon & Schuster.

Tyner, K. (1998). *Literacy in a digital world: Teaching and learning in the age of information.* Mahwah, NJ: Lawrence Erlbaum Associates.

Warnick, B. & Kline, S. L. (1992). The new rhetoric's argument schemes: A rhetorical view of practical reasoning. *Argumentation and Advocacy, 29,* 1–15.

Warnick, B. (1998a). Appearance or reality? Political parody on the Web in campaign '96. *Critical Studies in Mass Communication, 15,* 306–324.

Warnick, B. (1998b). Rhetorical criticism of public discourse on the Internet: Theoretical implications. *Rhetoric Society Quarterly, 28,* 73–84.

Weise, E. R. (1996). A thousand aunts with modems. In L. Cherny & E. R. Weise (Eds.), *Wired_women: Gender and new realities in cyberspace* (pp. vii–xv). Seattle, WA: Seal Press.

Welcome to WWWomen! (1997). Retrieved January 4, 1998 from the World Wide Web: wwwomen.com/about.shtml

Wertheim, M. (1996, March). Women, wake up about computers! *Glamour, 94,* 153.

What on Earth? A weekly look at trends, people and events around the world. (2000, January 22). *The Washington Post,* p. A13.

Whitcomb, C. (1996). Why aren't women on the Internet, really? *Arts and Letters* [Online serial]. Retrieved August 9, 1997 from the World Wide Web: www.bostonwomen.com/Whit.html

White, B. (2000, March 19). Online balloting: A question of fairness. *The Washington Post* [Online]. Retrieved June 27, 2000 from the World Wide Web: http://washingtonpost.com/wp-dyn/politics/A37369-2000Mar18.html

Winner, L. (1995, May–June). Peter Pan in cyberspace: Wired magazine's political vision. *Educom Review, 30* [Online]. Retrieved August 15, 1999 from the World Wide Web: http://www.educause.edu/pub/er/review/review articles/ 30318.html

The wired diaries. (1999). *Wired, 7.01,* 97–101, 106–107, 112–113, 120–123, 126–127, 132–135.

Wolf, G. (1998, September). The world according to Woz. *Wired, 6.09,* 118–121, 178, 180, 182–185.

You Crazy! (2000). *Governor Bush welcomes you to his virtual campaign headquarters.* Retrieved August 3, 2000 from the World Wide Web: http://www.youcrazy. com/georgewbush/georgelaura/index.php3

Author Index

A

Allis, S., 59–60
Althusser, L., 7
Astor, G., 75

B

Bakhtin, M. M., 107–108
Barad, V., 76
Bayers, C., 28, 41, 53
Beato, G., 74
Bellah, R. N., 5
Bennahum, D. S., 26, 44
Berland, J., 38, 42
Bertelson, D. A., 7
Bimber, B., 93, 116
Bitzer, L. F., 73
Bizzell, P., 106
Boal, I. A., 123
Bolter, J. D., 7–8, 102, 110
Bonsell, D. G., 65
Borsook, P., 37
Brame, G. G., 72
Brockman, J., 20, 26
Bronson, P., 31–37, 39, 45
Brook, J., 123
Burke, K., 3, 31, 68–69
Butler, J., 7

C

Case, D., 26
Castells, M., 10, 45, 100

Chesebro, J. W., 7, 65
Cohen, E., 15, 111

D

Davis, R., 91, 93
Dawson, M., 10
DeLoach, A., 80–81
Dertouzos, M. L., 2
Doheny-Farina, S., 12–13, 65, 123

E

Erbring, L., 93
Exley, Z., 88, 92

F

Fisher, B., 89, 116, 119
Fisher, W. R., 4
Fost, D., 20
Foster, J. B., 10
Fraser, N., 66–67, 74
Fraunfelder, M., 28
Freund, J., 49
Friedman, T., 105
Fryer, B., 75

G

Gates, B., 5
Gibson, W., 72
Glassman, J., 72–73

Goetz, T., 20
Grusin, R., 7–8, 102, 110
Gurak, L. J., 6, 12–13, 65, 67, 117

H

Haraway, D., 57, 123
Heron, K., 27
Herring, S., 67
Herzberg, B., 106
Hobbs, R., 7, 13
Howe, P. J., 2
Hudes, K., 21
Hudson, D., 20–21, 23, 27

I

Ignatius, D., 60
Ivie, R. L., 121

J

Jamieson, K. H., 11
Johns, A., 44
Johnston, D. C., 124
Jordan, T., 10, 12–13, 20, 110, 124
Joy, B., 57–60

K

Kantrowitz, B., 67, 74
Katz, J., 49–50, 63–64
Kelly, K., 2, 28–30, 41
Kennedy, G., 24, 27
Kennedy, H., 101
Kenner, R., 52
Kirsner, S., 28, 53, 54, 56
Krizek, R. L., 50
Kubey, R., 7
Kurzweil, R., 19, 56

L

Ladd, D., 73, 79
Landow, G. P., 106, 108
Lanham, R. A., 65
Lazarus, D., 27

Lehman, P. D., 51
Leonard, A., 51–52
Leslie, J., 55
Lester, W., 96
Light, J. S., 86
Lohr, S., 45

M

Madsen, R., 5
Maloney, J., 21
Mantovani, G., 11
Margolis, M., 89, 116, 119
Marvin, C., 3
Mays, J., 49
McChesney, R. W., 5, 8–11
Merkle, R., 59
Michals, D., 72
Millar, M. S., 22
Miller, C. R., 4
Miller, L., 81–82
Miller, S. E., 3, 5, 10, 74, 110, 122–124
Mitra, A., 14–15, 111–112
Moran, S., 21
Morgan, J., 76

N

Nakayama, T. K., 50
Neal, T. M., 88, 94
Negroponte, N., 44
New London Group, 6–7, 15
Nicholas, R., 72
Nie, N. H., 93
Notess, G. R., 89

O

Ogilvy, J., 56
Olbrechts-Tyteca, L., 35, 39–40, 43,
        45, 69–71
Ong, W. J., 7
Ott, B. L., 106, 112

P

Parks, B., 51, 55
Paulsen, K., 56

Penn, S., 70
Perelman, C., 35, 39–40, 43, 45, 69–70
Platt, C., 49, 51, 53–54
Purdy, J. S., 21

R

Reiss, S., 28–30, 41
Resnick, D., 89, 91–92, 116, 119
Rheingold, H., 5, 19, 56, 91
Richardson, A., 82
Ricoeur, P., 30, 38
Ritsch, M., 88–89
Roach, M., 51, 55
Rochlin, G. I., 123–124
Rodino, M., 67
Rossetto, L., 26

S

Schlosser-Hall, C. C., 22, 25
Schuyler, N., 76
Schwartz, E. I., 28
Schwartz, J., 70, 72, 75
Segell, M , 72
Selfe, C. L., 8, 26, 116
Sheff, D., 52, 54
Sherman, A., 72–73, 75, 77–80
Shogren, L., 94
Siemaszko, C., 101
Simons, J., 21

Sinclair, C., 5, 72–73, 79–80
Sterling, B., 27, 51
Stone, A. R., 77–78
Stross, R. E., 61
Sullivan, W. M., 5
Sutton, L. A., 79
Swidler, A., 5

T

Taggart, S., 51
Talbott, S. L., 121–123
Tapscott, D., 5, 10, 121–122
Tetzlaff, D., 110
Thomas, S. G., 73, 76
Tipton, S. M., 5
Travis, M. A., 104, 108
Turkle, S., 11, 13, 64, 68, 123
Tyner, K., 6–7

W

Walter, C., 106, 112
Warnick, B., 11, 14, 65, 90, 105, 109
Weise, E. R., 19
Wertheim, M., 77, 81
Whitcomb, C., 74, 77
Winner, L., 21
Wolf, G., 28

Subject Index

A

African Americans
  appeals to, 76
  portrayals of, in *Wired*, 47–49, 54–55
Algore2000.org, 88, 95, 102, 106
Alliteration, 97
Argument, 123–124
  forms of, 13, 22
  types of, 16
Argument from model, 35, 40, 54, 64, 70,
    75–76, 116
  definition of, 16
  as used, 42
Artificial intelligence, 19, 27, 56, 59, 60,
    117–118
Asceticism, 36, 39, 55
Asian Americans, portrayals of, in *Wired*,
    47–48
Asians, portrayals of, in *Wired*, 47–48
Association, in argument, 40, 42, 69
Audience response, 16, 29, 39, 94, 105,
    109, 111–112, 117
Audio, 102–103, 119
Authorship, *see also* Ethos, 14

B

Bandwidth, 110
Breakup Girl, 84
Bush, George W., 87–88, 96–97, 111

C

Chinese, 54

Commonplaces, 103–104, 107, 112
Community, 12, 112, 116–117, 119
  among women, 75
  loss of, 122–123
  as text–based, 15
Computer gaming, 12, 74, 93, 107
Computer-mediated communication
    (CMC), 12, 65, 86
  benefits of, 74
  constraints on, 17, 91
  and politics, 91
Computer Professionals for Social
    Responsibility, 125
Computing technology
  anthropomorphizing, 41
  development of, 29
  the economy and, 2, 8, 25–27, 76,
    124
  and gender, 71, 73
  lack of resources for, 74, 76, 110,
    120
  quality of life and, 3, 8, 27, 60, 74,
    75
  skills required for, 78
  use of, 80, 83
Condé Nast Publications, 30, 50
Counternarrative, need for, 121,
    124–125
Credibility, *see* Ethos
Critical literacy, *see also* Literacy, 15,
    90, 127
  definition of, 6
Critical thinking, 24, 52, 120
Cybergrrls, 14, 78, 116–117
Cybergrrl Webstation, 78, 83–84

143

Cyborgs, 57, 124

D

Digital divide, 25, 118
Digital video, 51, 101–102, 119
Dissociation, 16, 27, 55, 64, 69–71, 81, 116
  definition of, 40
  function of, 42–45

E

Electronic Frontier Foundation, 125
E-mail, on political campaign sites, 92–93,
  119
Environment, and technology, 58
Epideictic, 24, 27–28, 39, 42, 51, 117
Ethical issues, 37, 54, 118
  of technology development, 56, 58
Ethos, 15, 66
Exigence, 73, 75
Exley, Zack, 87–88, 92, 109
E-zines, See Webzines

F

Fan out, 11
Figurative analogy, 40
Flaming, 85

G

Gender, see Women
Genetic engineering, 57, 59
Genre
  of appeals to women, 73
  definition of, 16
  in Wired's writing, 52, 54
  speech, 105, 107
GIF (Graphic Interchange Format), 101
Globalization, 54
Gore, Al, 96, 111
  contradictions in speech, 102
  image changes, 103
  misstatements of, 100
  speeches of, 98–99
gURL, 84

gwbush.com, 87–89, 92, 94–95, 101,
  103–104, 109
  popularity of, 89

H

Heteroglossia, 107
Hierarchical appeals
  definition of, 4
  use of, 5, 55, 68, 80
Hierarchy, double, 27, 43
Human-computer interaction, 1, 12
Hypertext, 14, 104, 108, 112, 119

I

Identity construction, 35, 42, 66, 68,
  80
Institute for Social Assessment of
  Information Technology,
  125
Interactivity on political websites,
  92, 107, 111, 119
Internet
  access to, 92
  benefits of, 75
  changes in, 90–91, 120
  civic life on, 89, 119
  demographics, 17, 22, 45–46, 64,
    67, 110, 124
  politics and, 88, 90
  portrayals of, 72
  regulation of, 9, 25, 81, 90,
    109–110
  uses of, 85–86, 93, 125
Internet Policy Institute, 126
Interpellation, 7, 66, 70–71
  definition of, 67
Intertextuality, 13–14, 90, 108, 119
  community and, 17
  definition of, 105, 107
  use of 105, 112

J

Joy, Bill, 29–30, 56

L

Latinas, portrayal of, in *Wired*, 47–48
Libertarianism, 16, 24–28, 39, 44, 48, 55,
  60, 82
  ideology of, 10, 19–20, 42, 124
Libertarian Party, 20
Link patterns, 109
Literacy, *see also* Critical literacy
  aural and oral, 7
  Internet, 74, 123
  media, 7, 11, 13
  print and alphabetic, 122

M

Malapropisms, 101
Masculinization, 79–82, 86
Media
  convergence, 102
  ownership, 9
  policy, 12, 18, 125–126
  reform, 10, 60
  representation, 13, 116, 126–127
Metaphor, 12, 14, 22, 40, 55, 64, 69, 80
  clusters of, 41, 121
  definition of, 41
  frontier, 77, 79, 86
  use of, 5, 27, 53
Microcinema, 52
Microsoft Windows NT, 29
Minx, 84
Moore's Law, 3–4
Multiliteracies, 7
Multimedia, 101–102, 108

N

Nanotechnology, 57, 59
Narrative, 14, 96, 120
  function of, 31
  structure, 16, 22, 28, 38, 66, 117
  time in, 38, 55
  use of, 8, 13, 25, 27, 35, 81, 104, 116
Net Chick, 79
new media, 53, 122
  characteristics of, 11
  types of, 10
New York Times, The, 54–55
Nisenholtz, Martin, 54–55
Nostalgia, 44, 122–123

P

Parody, 105, 109, *see also*
  Political parody
  definition of, 89
  visual, 96
Pastiche, 11, 103
People for Internet Responsibility, 126
Persuasion, 14, 85, 112
  appeals to audience, 4
  in public discourse, 3
  strategies, 17, 116
Political parody, 14, 87, 90, 94
  coherence in, 106
  persuasion and, 17
  role in campaigns, 89
  strategies of, 95, 104
  use of media reports, 88, 111
Political participation, 93, 111
Portal, 88, 109
Postfeminism, 78–79, 85
Presence, in argument, 70
Presidential candidates, character of,
  96, 98
Pseudo speech, 98
Public discourse
  absence of debate in, 9, 41–42, 60,
    120, 126
  addressed to women, 65
  as fabricated, 96, 99–100
  hierarchical appeals in, 69
  ideology in, 14
  predictions in, 4–5, 122
  technology and, 3–4, 8, 116
  values in, 6

R

Race, *Wired's* views on, 48–50
Relinquishment, 58–59
Rhetoric
  deliberative, 24, 27, 121

Rhetoric (*continued*)
  and knowledge construction, 124
  patterns in, 3, 108
  pejorative sense of, 64
Rhetorical criticism, 18, 65, 69, 86, 90
  as analysis, 12–18, 22, 111
  critical framing and, 15
  definition of, 7
Robotics, 57
Rossetto, Louis, 19, 23, 26, 50

S

Sexism, 37
Social isolation, 123
Stereotypes, 55, 81, 118
Style
  definition of, 15
  and persuasion, 66
  in *Wired*'s writing, 39

T

Techno evolutionism, 38
Technological elite, 6, 56, 60, 82
  as role models, 24, 64, 116–117
Technology
  future of, 51, 122, 126
  and politics, 63, 126
Technophobia, 123
Teenagers, appeals to, 84
Textuality, use in parody, 104, 106
Transparency
  definition of, 10
  of media representations, 11–12

U

United States, as global leader, 8, 26, 32

V

Value pairs, 42–45, 70
Values, clusters of, 55, 118–119
Venture capitalism, 32, 36, 39
Virtual reality, 60
Voter interests, 90, 93, 96
Voting online, 94

W

Web browsing, 105
Websites, official vs. parodic, 101
Webzines, 77, 82–83
Whiteness, 50
Whole Earth 'Lectronic Link
    (WELL), 19
Wireless technology, 53
Wired magazine, 11, 63
  content of, 51
  distinctiveness, 22
  diversity in coverage, 38, 118
  ideology of, 10, 16, 24–28, 31–32,
    45, 55
  predictions in, 1–2, 25, 51, 56–60
  purpose of, 21, 23
  readership, 5, 16, 20, 22–23, 25, 41,
    45, 116, 118
  rhetoric of, 35
  staff, 21, 50
Wired Ventures, Inc., 22–21, 26
Women
  appeals to, 66, 72, 75, 77, 85
  as consumers, 67
  portrayals of, 33, 37, 43, 46–48, 55
  technology and, 17
World Wide Web, *see also* Internet
  as broadcast medium, 91–92
  changes in, 108
  rhetorical features of, 109